Be the Greatest Product Manager Ever

**MASTER SIX PROVEN SKILLS
TO GET THE CAREER YOU WANT**

Lewis C. Lin

Impact Interview

Seattle, Washington

Published by Impact Interview, 115 North 85th St., Suite 202, Seattle, WA 98103.

Several fictitious examples have been used in this book; these examples involve names of real people, places and organizations. Any slights of people, places, or organizations are unintentional.

The author and publisher have made every effort to ensure the accuracy and completeness of information contained in this book. However, we assume no responsibility for errors, inaccuracies, omissions, or any inconsistency herein.

Corporations, organizations and educational institutions: bulk quantity pricing is available. For information, contact lewis@impactinterview.com.

SECOND EDITION / Sixth Printing

Lin, Lewis C.
Be the Greatest Product Manager Ever: Six Steps to Getting the Career You Want / Lewis C. Lin

ALSO BY LEWIS C. LIN

Career

Be the Greatest Product Manager Ever

Interview Preparation

Case Interview Questions for Tech Companies

Decode and Conquer

The Marketing Interview

The Product Manager Interview

Secrets of the Product Manager Interview

Negotiation

71 Brilliant Salary Negotiation Email Samples

Contents

Believe you can and you're halfway there.

THEODORE ROOSEVELT

Introduction

It's a Playbook

The best leaders create and use playbooks to improve personal and team performance. John Wooden, one of the greatest basketball coaches ever, had his Pyramid of Success playbook. Brené Brown, the author of five #1 New York Times bestsellers, has *Dare to Lead*. And Stephen Covey has *The 7 Habits of Highly Effective People* playbook. These playbooks help us remember and focus on the most impactful skills.

Similarly, the ESTEEM™ framework is my playbook for being successful in all career stages, starting from PM to CEO.

It's based on my observations, research, and personal journey as my career progressed from Google to Microsoft, which culminated in my being one of the youngest Fortune 100 executives at age 32.

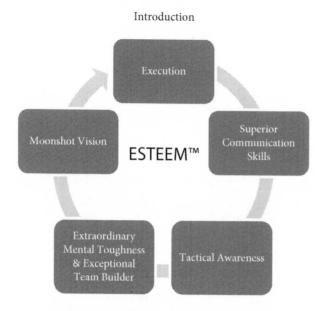

I use the ESTEEM™ framework when:

- Hiring new talent
- Helping my direct reports grow professionally
- Setting expectations for myself on what it means to be a great CEO while being a PM at heart

Why You Need This Book

McKinsey tells us that a whopping 65 percent of product managers don't know what it takes to advance in their organization. And only 35 percent of product managers feel they have enough coaching and mentoring to help them move up.[1]

My personal experience reflects McKinsey's insights; many of my managers didn't know how to coach:

- My boss at Citibank wanted to send 30 emails and asked me to draft them on her behalf. Her explanation why I couldn't send

---

[1] The Product Management Talent Dilemma by McKinsey

my emails to the recipients directly: "Lewis, nobody knows who you are!" It felt like my boss wanted to take credit for my work. This episode demonstrated the importance of clear *communication*. I would have been more accepting if she simply said, "I'm very busy. Lewis, can you draft these emails to save me time?"

- My next boss: he dreamed of becoming a religious missionary. He believed starting and then cashing out a tech startup was the best way to fund his religious aspirations. The startup failed six months later. It's no surprise; tech startups have a low success rate of ten percent. There are better ways to get rich quick. His fantasy demonstrated how critical it is to have *tactical awareness*.

- At Microsoft, my first boss tossed around corporate clichés like "Skate to where the puck is going, not where it has been." Like all platitudes, the *why* is clear. However, his cliché was ineffective because it wasn't actionable. In other words, he missed his chance to explain *how* I could know "where the puck is going?" This story shows that *building a team* is more than parroting famous sports quotes.

Your experience likely reflects mine: many bosses have good intentions, but they are not career development experts. So, you can't expect your boss to manage your career for you. You'll have to manage it yourself.

This book reveals the advice I wish my bosses dispensed but never did. You'll learn about the six core capabilities – from the ESTEEM™ Method – you need to advance your career. To help you master those six capabilities, I'll share effective yet rarely mentioned tactics.

What I Won't Cover

In this book, I won't spend any time discussing how to:

- Conduct user interviews
- Write requirements
- Manage a backlog
- Create a roadmap
- Run a daily stand-up meeting

There are a few reasons why. First, there are many resources, available on the web, that cover this in detail. Second, hiring managers know that the greatest PMs are distinguished by their soft skills. The world's greatest leaders – Steve Jobs, Jeff Bezos, Elon Musk – their legacies certainly weren't built on their abilities to conduct user interviews or run daily stand-up meetings. Instead, their greatness was based on something else altogether: the six competencies of the ESTEEM™ framework.

The ESTEEM™ framework evolved through my research and observations of high-performing product managers and tech leaders. No matter the PM career stage – individual contributor, CEO, or somewhere between – these competencies reveal top-performers.

Caveats

As you start reading, you may groan at my advice and say:

- Take notes? I don't need a book to tell me that.
- Follow the chain of command? Ridiculous. Elon Musk is the greatest PM ever, and he doesn't respect any chain, whether it's the S.E.C. or his board of directors.

If that's you, you may be taking my advice out of context. There are important nuances and takeaways that, at first glance, appear to be trivial. John Wooden, our aforementioned college basketball coach, is famously known for coaching his players on how to wear their socks. Of all the things that Wooden could discuss, life, leadership, and basketball, there must be better things to dwell on. But those who internalized his teachings found that wearing socks correctly was the first step to better performance. Why? Wearing socks correctly meant fewer blisters. And fewer blisters meant healthy, uninjured players.

You'll also find the ESTEEM™ framework works best for PMs in large organizations. To thrive in a large organization, one must be skilled at navigating formal processes, influencing sister organizations, and winning the political game. Some PMs will find some of my tactics to be less applicable because politics, processes, and hierarchies are less prominent in smaller organizations.

Book Convention and Use of Gendered Pronouns

For simplicity, I'll refer to bosses as she or her. Everyone else, I'll refer to as he or him. If you haven't concluded already, I am blunt, and I will not hold back. I will be tough and critical of bosses, just as I will be tough and critical of non-bosses. It doesn't mean I'm anti-female or anti-male!

Let's get going. There's no time to waste.

Lewis C. Lin

CHAPTER 1

Journey from Product Manager to CEO

You'll need to know the PM career path before I delve into the six competencies. I've distilled that path down to five distinct job levels from PM to CEO; let's review those now.

Level 1: Product Manager

You start level 1 with responsibility for a feature. As a level 1 product manager, depending on the company, you'll have titles like:

Amazon	Product Manager
	Senior Product Manager
	Principal Product Manager
Facebook	Rotational Product Manager
	Product Manager
Google	Associate Product Manager
	Product Manager

	Senior Product Manager
Microsoft	Program Manager 1, 2
	Senior Program Manager[2]
	Principal Program Manager
Uber	Associate Product Manager
	Product Manager 1, 2
	Senior Product Manager 1, 2

You write requirements and talk to customers. You run the weekly meetings and work with engineers to prioritize features. Your immediate teams find you helpful. Your boss is content with your contributions. You're getting things done and your collaborators say good things about you.

Outside of your immediate team, people don't know much about you. Others assume you're getting your job done, but you're certainly not a company-wide thought-leader.

Your boss doesn't assign complex projects to you. You don't have the experience or confidence yet to deal with complicated projects, especially with hordes of stakeholders.

You're frustrated that you haven't gotten promoted. You're smart and capable, but your boss hasn't clarified what you need to do to get to the next level.

Level 2: Group Product Manager

---

[2] Microsoft does use the "Product Manager" title. However, most professionals believe Microsoft's "Program Manager" title is closer to the industry's definition of PM.

As a level 2 group product manager, depending on the company, you'll have titles like:

Amazon	Senior Product Manager[3]
	Manager, Product Management
	Sr. Manager, Product Management
Facebook	Product Manager[3]
Google	Senior Product Manager[3]
	Group Product Manager
Microsoft	Senior Program Manager Lead
	Principal Program Manager Lead
	Principal Group Program Manager
Uber	Senior Product Manager 1, 2[3]
	Group Product Manager

You've been promoted to manager, and you have direct reports. You've earned a reputation for getting things done, and people outside of your team have heard of your work.

At meetings, you're treated as a senior member and given the respect that comes with it.

You've also got a reputation for being a skilled communicator. When your boss can't present at executive meetings, you stand-in for her. You're not as good, but executives are impressed with your presentation skills from time-to-time.

---

[3] These titles can be given to both individual contributors (level 1) or front-line managers (level 2).

Managing direct reports is a new challenge. Your directs may like you as a person. However, you're not their favorite boss ever, unless you've found time to coddle them.

You're getting some slightly bigger projects, but game-changing, once-in-a-lifetime initiatives are typically driven at the VP, or sometimes director, level.

Level 3: Director of Product Management

Kudos! You've made it to level 3. Depending on the company, at this level, you'll have titles like:

Amazon	Director, Product Management
Facebook	Director, Product Management
	Sr. Director, Product Management
Google	Director, Product Management
	Sr. Director, Product Management
Microsoft	Partner Director, Program Management
Uber	Director, Product Management
	Sr. Director, Product Management

You stand a little straighter and hold your head a little higher. Why? The title "Director" has a nice ring to it; it carries gravitas.

You're now a manager of managers; you're leading a bigger team! Managing others is no longer new; you're piecing together what it means to manage a team.

Your communication skills are even more refined now; some say you have executive presence.

People realize you're different:

- You anticipate problems others miss.
- You get things done more efficiently and elegantly.
- You think about problems in a unique way.
- You connect with executives, customers, and partners seamlessly.

You don't always get primary responsibility for game-changing initiatives, but you're often the trusted lieutenant for the person who does.

When you change roles, you have success recruiting one, maybe two, old contacts onto your new team.

Level 4: VP of Product Management

At level 4 you've made it to the CEO's inner circle, or you're close to it. Your organization now spans a team of about 20 to 100 people.

If you've made it this far, you have mental toughness, the ability to build teams, or both.

CEOs love tapping you for VP roles because you can replenish depleted departments with your far-reaching network. And when you bring over trusted protégés, they are senior enough that they, in turn, augment your organization by recruiting one or two of their own.

You may have a knack for inheriting teams that others have branded as mediocre and installing new processes, training, and culture to improve performance.

You may be the person that's made corporate history like the person who made Amazon Prime a reality or established Android's market share dominance.

When someone else sets the vision, you fulfill it. Audacious visions are hard to implement, but you succeed because your toughness has no equal.

Sometimes, the company needs a fresh vision because growth has stagnated or declined. Your CEO wants you to deliver a new vision. You try, and you fail.

You buy one instead. First by hiring a "strategy" person for your team and then engaging with McKinsey, but neither works.

Level 5: CEO

As CEO, you're at Level 5. You're the boss until you realize you're not. You now have multiple bosses called "the board." Forming alliances and managing personalities, something you started to cultivate and hone at Level 3, now really matter.

Steering the company to where it needs to go is difficult. Your company's consensus-based approach makes it hard to take quick and decisive action. You try an authoritative approach instead, which then alienates rank-and-file employees.

You're a symbolic figurehead. You make token appearances at critical crises, but you do not play a critical role.

However, if you're the best of the best – like Steve Jobs, Jeff Bezos, and Elon Musk – you know the most important thing you can do is provide a moonshot vision that will create a revolutionary, new business that will guarantee profits and growth for your company's next 30 years.

CHAPTER 2

Introducing the
ESTEEM Method™

If the journey from PM to CEO is where you want to go, there are six capabilities you need to master.

I've created a handy six-letter acronym to make it easy to remember: ESTEEM™. If you want to make it to the top, you'll need ESTEEM™ (pun intended). Here are the components:

Execution
Superior communication skills
Tactical awareness
Extraordinary mental toughness
Exceptional team builder
Moonshot vision

1 Execution

The first competency is execution. If a PM can't deliver a feature, product, or otherwise *get things done*, what's the point?

The best execution-oriented PMs can do anywhere from five to ten times the work of an ordinary PM. They have a supernatural ability to get things done. That talented PM's productivity is the reason for the team's happiness. Without him or her, the team would bend and (likely) break under the collective workload.

Managers have no problem giving the best PMs merit bonuses. No one is jealous because those PMs earned it.

2   Superior Communication Skills

The second competency is superior communication skills.

Usually starting at the group product manager level, the best PMs tell captivating stories during critical times such as:

- Executive meetings
- Product brainstorms
- Brown bag presentations
- Sales conferences

Sometimes they tell stories with intelligence, filled with facts, numbers, or logic. Other times they tell stories with charm, developing chemistry and rapport. And the best can tell stories with heart, tugging on emotions and revealing authenticity.

During promotion time, they are hard to miss. Superior communicators get promoted at an unprecedented rate.

Superior communicators remind promotion committees of well-known CEOs like Jeff Bezos, Satya Nadella, and Elon Musk. Not all CEOs are competent, but all famous CEOs communicate exceptionally. And there's a good reason why: CEOs must communicate effectively with their employees, customers, partners, and shareholders.

3 Tactical Awareness

The third competency is tactical awareness.

It's a term I borrowed from soccer. The military also uses the term tactical awareness, which likely evolved from a more popular term "situational awareness."

Those unfamiliar with the world of soccer can get thrown off by the phrase tactical awareness. They think I'm referring to rote execution or operational work.

That's not what I mean. Tactical awareness is about:

1. Assessing the situation.
2. Making good decisions, based on that assessment.

In soccer, a player exhibits tactical awareness by:

1. Understanding where the nearest attacker or defender is.
2. Predicting where he is going to pass the ball.
3. Realizing where his teammates are and where they should be.
4. Knowing where he is and where he needs to be.
5. Making the right decision to stop the attacker or elude the defender.

In product management, tactical awareness is about utilizing other-worldly tactics that allow the best, usually starting at the director level, to:

1. Understanding what needs to be done.
2. Foreseeing how others will react.
3. Laying out how to achieve the goal.
4. Making correct decisions – on the appropriate behaviors, deliverables, resources, and allies – to get the right outcomes.

Tactical awareness is what many call the "sixth sense." That is, as you get closer to the top, it's no longer enough to work extra hours; almost everyone does that. Instead, you need tactical awareness; it is what people mean when they say you need to "work smarter."

4   Extraordinary Mental Toughness

The fourth competency is extraordinary mental toughness.

Many can execute, but few can lead groundbreaking change. Seismic change happens when a PM leader stomachs daunting circumstances and grinds through long hours.

They don't quit. Even if they failed 999 times, they're ready to try the thousandth time, and so on.

Ordinary PMs aren't the ones building billion-dollar businesses, inventing self-driving cars, or challenging long-held taxi regulations. The ordinary wilt when there's a hint of resistance, whether it's a stubborn engineer or an executive bully.

Great products are great because they're hard to build. And many PMs don't want to do hard things.

5   Exceptional Team Builder

The fifth competency is exceptional team builder. The best, usually starting at the VP level, call upon their deep network to quickly fill PM openings.

But that's not the only thing that makes them outstanding. These team builders can and love to teach others how to do their jobs well, and they expect their direct reports to do the same.

6 Moonshot Vision

The sixth competency is moonshot vision.

Many CEOs communicate well, operate businesses efficiently, and demonstrate reasonable business judgment. But legendary CEOs differentiate themselves with moonshot vision. A moonshot vision is a bold product vision that feels like John F. Kennedy's 1961 proclamation to land the first humans on the moon.

Moonshot CEOs typically meet three criteria. They:

1. Propose a moonshot vision or idea that is unique, audacious, and extraordinary.
2. Describe why that vision will meet a large, profitable need.
3. Persuade, even skeptics, why the vision is feasible and, if necessary, the specific steps to build it now.

CHAPTER 3

Skill 1: Execution

Regardless of your title, your boss hired you to get things done. We call that execution. Some of us are exponentially better at executing than others, and it starts with what you do on day one.

1 How to Start Every New Job

Type A personalities charge into new situations. They speak up and propose ideas. They want to be promoted not just quickly, but now. They get discouraged when the situation isn't what they expected. If you're reading this book, you are likely a type A.

Instead of indulging a type A routine, start your new role by **pausing your ambition (and judgment) for 90 days**. Co-workers get annoyed by the new know-it-all, and the boss can't help but get irritated by newcomers who demand to get promoted when they haven't yet proven themselves. And contrary to what oblivious newcomers believe, instead of helping the team, they are typically hurting it!

What to do instead? Observe, instead of judge. Don't complain about tools, processes, or co-workers. Instead, stay in the present. Get familiar with your new surroundings. Fit in, rather than stick out.

As you inch toward your 90-day mark, you'll get a better sense of when to speak up and what to propose. You'll also have a chance to prove yourself and letting others see your worth.

2 How to Figure Out What to Do

It's easy to get overwhelmed as a PM. Accountability weighs on your shoulders, and you can feel like you must do everything. The endless number of stakeholders – ranging from engineering to marketing – makes it even harder to figure out who to attend to first. You're not alone if you feel like everyone is your boss.

Alternatively, you may feel like you have nothing to do. Your boss is too busy to give you projects. Or your organization defines PM poorly. Your engineers and designers don't ask for your help because they don't know what or how you're supposed to help.

Either way, don't overthink your day-to-day priorities. **Ask your boss what you need to work on.** And if she doesn't have an opinion, then put yourself in her shoes and ask yourself the following:

1. What does your boss care about most?
2. Who needs my output to be effective?
3. How can I help them get what they need to be done?
4. What unique strengths and superpowers can I share?

3 How Stuff Gets Done: Understanding Why System 1 and 2 Affects Your Work

System 1 thinking is reactive thinking.

System 2 thinking is thoughtful thinking.

System 1 activates anytime you're trying to get things done like powering through emails or rushing out the door to begin your morning commute. You want it done fast so you can move onto the next checklist item. You don't need to think about what or how to do it because you've done it before.

System 1 is also responsible for other default and thoughtless behaviors:

Default System 1 Action	Unexplored System 2 Blind Spot
Saying yes to the boss...	Because we've never said no.
Monetizing with online advertising only...	Because we've never tried a monthly subscription model.
Avoiding building desktop software...	Because the company has only built mobile apps.

Most of us don't need to improve our System 1 skills. We are well-practiced with System 1 because it's our fight-or-flight survival instinct.

Why does System 2 matter?

In today's fast-paced world, many of us try to do as much as possible. As a result, we default to System 1. We're good at System 1 because we do it all the time.

System 2 happens when we're not trying to be quick. It happens when we have time. Maybe it's an hour, three hours, or three days. Thinking becomes slower, relaxed, and most importantly, pensive.

Given our busy lives, we rarely perform System 2 thinking. System 2 is:

- **Creative thinking** to innovate new features vs. copying the competition.
- **Analytical thinking** to analyze customer data vs. delegating to another team.
- **Logical thinking** to influence a course of action vs. bullying, shaming, or intimidating to get action.
- **Empathetic thinking** to explain why we missed our goals vs. blaming or making excuses.

How to get better at System 2 thinking?

All of us could use more System 2 thinking and *get better* at it. Here's how:

1. **Awareness.** You can only stop your System 1 response if you're aware that it's on. When System 1 is running, your heart beats faster. You're more alert and you're more likely to be impatient. Who has time for patience when you've got to react to survive?

2. **Evaluate.** Is System 1 appropriate for the task? Or is System 2 more correct?

3. **Resist.** If you need System 2, turn off your default System 1 response. Don't respond to a roadmap request that you're unprepared to answer. Instead, buy time (for System 2) with this response: "I haven't yet updated our roadmap for this coming quarter. We're planning to get it done next month. In the meantime, can I send you the roadmap from last quarter?"

Here's one more tip: **write write write.** Stephen Sinofsky once said, "Writing is thinking," and one of my favorite authors says that "Writing is about learning to pay attention." Andy Grove is also a fan of writing reports, and Amazon initiates System 2 thinking by having meeting participants read memos for the first half-hour.

To summarize, writing activates System 2 by forcing us to slow, focus, and sharpen our thinking. If a colleague blurts out a System 1-led half-thought, help him activate his System 2 by suggesting that he send you a written proposal.

When should we do System 1 and System 2 tasks?

Do System 2 tasks earlier in the day, when rest and strong coffee can get us through tasks requiring concentration and creativity.

Do System 1 tasks later in the day. System 1 tasks are those you've performed previously, which don't require the same amount of concentration or willpower.

4 Just Do and Update

Some believe that they are demonstrating initiative if they are busy. Unfortunately, being busy doesn't always mean taking initiative.

Before I explain the nuances of taking initiative, let me describe, from a manager's point of view, why initiative is so important.

Why is initiative important?

Product managers who lack initiative must be prompted *what to do* and *when to do it*. Having to remind their directs annoys managers.

A big part of getting promoted is being likable. Those who annoy managers are not likely to get promoted.

What are the different types of initiative?

I've created an acronym WARDD™ to easily recall the five initiative types. That is, use WARDD™ to ward off your boss' wrath.

Wait
Ask
Recommend
Do
Do & update

Type 1: Wait

This should be self-explanatory. Waiting does not show initiative.

Type 2: Ask

Asking for projects sounds like initiative, but it's not. It simply signals that you're available for work.

Type 3: Recommend

Now it starts to get nuanced.

Some bosses like receiving recommendations. They may not have the time, creativity, or problem-solving skills to come up with their own solutions. They will gladly take all the recommendations they can get.

Other bosses hesitate when receiving recommendations. It's not because they like the sound of their own voice, although that may sometimes be the case. It's more that not all recommendations are relevant or valuable.

Going further, all proposals – valuable or not – place the burden of decision-making and accountability onto bosses. It adds yet another item on their never-ending to-do list. Furthermore, while it doesn't take much effort to simply say yes to a proposal, it's significantly more work to reject a proposal, explain why, and deal with hurt feelings.

Type 4: Do

Type 4 does away with the intermediate step of getting bosses' permission. Bosses save time, mental effort, and the burden of decision-making. It's beautiful when a direct report simply does the right thing, and bosses can sit back and relax. Why else would hiring managers covet those who are "independent" and "self-starters?"

Nevertheless, here are *some* bosses who prefer that you recommend and ask for permission first.

Perhaps your bosses are micromanagers. However, in my experience, it's usually less about your bosses and more about you. They may be uncomfortable with you taking unilateral action because they don't trust your judgment. Which is another way of saying: your proposal is not appropriate. If that's you, then you have some work to do. Learn to make stronger proposals by improving your knowledge, experience, and judgment. You will be trusted to operate at type 4 initiative soon enough.

One last thing: it may be that your judgment is perfectly tuned, and your bosses believe in your capabilities, but they still prefer that you ask for permission. In those cases, I've found that the problem lies with your co-workers and culture. That is, your co-workers exhibit weak judgment. As a result, the culture has morphed to institute checks and balances to prevent those with weak judgment from summoning catastrophe.

Type 5: Do and update.

When I say, "Do and update," I mean update *proactively.* Type 5 has all the benefits of type 4 plus proactive updates. For bosses, type 5 initiative is nirvana.

Why proactive updates make a difference

We can appreciate proactive communication patterns by exploring why reactive communication patterns can be detrimental. Communicating reactively can:

- *Induce anxiety and fear,* especially if your bosses don't know what's going on
- *Destroy trust,* particularly if your bosses feel like you're sneaking around behind their back and pursuing personal agendas
- *Create more work,* especially if the boss feels like they must hunt you down for updates

Trust is the foundation of a good relationship with your boss. Don't risk damaging your relationship with a reactive communication pattern. Strengthen your relationship by communicating proactively.

Why Bosses Love Those Who "Do and Update"

One last look at why type 5 initiative is the best form of initiative, I constructed a table summarizing the benefits to bosses. Long story short: bosses love PMs who save them time and effort.

Type	Time Spent	Mental Effort	Decision-Making Effort
Wait	High	High	Low
Ask	High	High	Low

Recommend	Depends[4]	High	High
Do	Low	Medium	Low
Do & update	Low	Low	Low

Inspired by Stephen Covey

5 The Importance of Visibility

Your colleagues, especially your boss, want to know what you're working on and the results you've achieved. They won't know until you've told them. If you don't tell them, they'll imagine the worst.

Don't expect others to ask for updates. Repeatedly requesting updates feels like a chore. So be proactive. Update early and often.

What to Include in Your Visibility Updates

Status	"You asked for a new product roadmap, and it's still on my to-do list. Earlier this week, I was busy with the developer conference, but I'm still on target to get you the new draft by Tuesday afternoon."
Results	"I have results from the Gizmo A/B test. The new Gizmo feature increases weekly revenue by five percent."
Learnings	"Here are the top three learnings from the product conference..."
Action Items	"Just a reminder, here are the top two action items I need from you..."
Plans	"There are five phases to the Gizmo launch. Aarushi is spearheading phase one, with a completion date of June 30..."

---

[4] Good recommendations don't take up bosses' time, but bad recommendations can increase it.

Deliverables	"Slide 14 will show average income going up, but revenue per user going down. We're 80 percent confident of our hypothesis; finance will have the actual numbers for us on Friday."

How to Provide Visibility

There are many ways to provide visibility:

- **Email.** CC or forward important email threads. If the email thread is hard to follow, add a summary before forwarding, or draft a new email from scratch.
- **Meeting.** Organize a meeting. Or use informal meetings, such as the office drop-by, for quick updates.
- **Drafts and outlines.** Whether it's a Word document or PowerPoint presentation, share drafts, even imperfect ones, so your audience can see where you're headed.
- **Project plans.** Project plans should contain clear deliverables, milestones, and progress to date.

Don't worry about providing too much visibility. Most people would rather you over-communicate than not communicate at all. If the email volume is too much, trust that they will tell you. Or they might be okay deleting any email updates they don't have time to read.

6   Multitasking Doesn't Work

Some of us multitask better than others, but here's the one thing you need to know:

Multitasking hurts productivity and increases mental fatigue. Don't do it.

7 Follow the Chain of Command

Never go over or around your boss. Always inform your boss when you intend to operate around her. Secret one-on-one meetings, either with your boss' boss or other senior individuals, will raise suspicion.

If your boss' boss asks you to do something, don't automatically say yes. Inform your boss first and ask for their permission. If you fail to do so, your boss can feel betrayed.

Here are some inspirational phrases you could use while still being assertive:

- "I understand that you don't like the idea. Do you mind if I do one last check with engineering? They'll probably feel the same way as you do, but I'd like to check if you don't object."
- "I wanted to let you know I chatted with ___ about a ___ role. Nothing will likely come out of it, but I wanted to let you know in case they contact you about it."

Extend the same courtesy to your peers. Follow rules and processes. Inform your peers when you intend to break from convention. They value loyalty too.

CHAPTER 4

Skill 2: Superior Communication Skills

The best communicators use frameworks to share, captivate, and influence effectively. First, I'll introduce a framework favored by McKinsey consultants: Situation-Complication-Resolution. Then I'll review Steve Jobs' favorite communication frameworks including the Rule of Three. Lastly, I'll share a tip on how you can be authoritative like a professor.

1 Use Situation-Complication-Resolution (SCR)

As a product manager, influencing is the key to getting things done.

But where do you start? How much context is too much? How much is too little? And most importantly, what's a surefire approach that will work every time?

Popular with McKinsey consultants, SCR is an effective way to present a solution to a problem. Here's how it works:

Situation

Share an unbiased view of current conditions. Capturing your audience's attention is key; your situational recap should:

- Be relevant
- Feel familiar
- Be consistent with their beliefs

Complication

Complication is the twist that implores the listener to give the situation some additional thought.

In the SCR framework, the complication section is often dramatic or tension-filled, which makes it easier to spot. Here are some situation-complication examples:

Tension-building element	Example
New competitor	"Apple just launched the iPhone. Our own engineers, here at Blackberry, claimed last week that the iPhone wasn't doable (*situation*). **Thanks to Apple, our 10-year roadmap is now outdated** (*complication*)."
Changing business conditions	"We took out a $1B loan under the assumption that the market would grow at 15% per year. The recession hit, and our business is shrinking (*situation*). **We will have to lay off 5,000 people to avoid default, unless we sell some divisions** (*complication*)."

Resolution

This step proposes a solution to the complication. The resolution is presented with urgency, with the hope of compelling the audience to action.

Here are some examples to illustrate the SCR framework. They come from *Time Magazine*, describing the best inventions of the year. It proves that SCR is not just popular with McKinsey consultants. It's popular everywhere.

SCR Examples

	Situation	Complication	Resolution
New Dolls (Barbie)	For 57 years, the world's most famous doll has been stick-thin.	Studies show [this was a] damaging beauty standard for generations of young women.	This changed in January when Mattel decided to make Barbie look more like the girls who play with her. [Barbie] now has three additional body types: petite, tall and curvy.
New Drones (DJI)	In recent years, drones have become smarter flyers, faster	But for the most part, they're still too big and bulky to carry around comfortably,	Not so with DJI's Mavic Pro, which debuted in September; it's got

	racers, and better photographers.	which can turn off more-casual consumers.	all the trimmings of a state-of-the-art drone—obstacle-avoidance technology, a 4K camera and the ability to track subjects while -flying— but it can also fold down to the size of a loaf of bread, smaller than any of its competitors.
New Solar Roofs (Tesla)	[Solar panels] help the environment and save money.	[But you] litter your roof with bulky metal boxes. That's the dilemma home-solar-panel buyers have faced for years.	Tesla's response: the Solar Roof, a series of tiles designed to blend together while also harnessing the power of the sun.

Source: Time Magazine

Examples: Situation-Resolution (SR)

Sometimes the SCR framework doesn't fit cleanly. It's okay to just use situation-resolution (SR) and bypass the complication.

	Situation	Resolution
Hyperadapt 1.0 (Nike)	Almost everyone who sees Back to the Future wants three things: a time-traveling DeLorean, a working hoverboard and a pair of self-lacing shoes.	Now, thanks to Nike, the shoe dream is a reality. When wearers press a button near the tongue, the Hyper-Adapt 1.0s automatically tighten and loosen around their foot.
Bolt Electric Vehicle (Chevrolet)	For most buyers, electric vehicles fall into two camps: too expensive (think the $66,000 Tesla Model S) and too limited (the Nissan Leaf gets just 100 miles per charge).	General Motors aims to bridge that gap with the Chevrolet Bolt, which touts crowd-pleasing features, like more than 200 miles of driving on a single charge, at a relatively low cost.

Source: Time Magazine

One last historical note: the SCR framework is a more memorable version of Barbara Minto's SCQA framework (situation-complication-question-answer) featured in her book, *The Minto Pyramid Principle*.

2   Use Zippy Words

Memorable words matter

Zippy is a Steve Jobs term for eye-catching and memorable words. Consider these popular Apple phrases:

- *Insanely great.*
- *Think different.*

Or these quotes:

- *We're here to put a dent in the universe.*
- *iPod Shuffle is smaller and lighter than a pack of gum.*
- *Do you want to spend the rest of your life selling sugared water or do you want a chance to change the world?*

You might say, "Meh. This is marketing." If so, you probably hate advertising, buzz words, and jargon as well.

I hate buzzwords and jargon too, but marketing matters. As a PM, you'll need to get buy-in from others. And to get buy-in, your proposal must:

1. **Catch one's attention**. Competing teams will clamor your stakeholders for their time, attention, and buy-in.
2. **Remain memorable**. Nothing will happen to an idea that's forgotten.
3. **Be easy to share**. You'll need allies to help fight for your proposal. Your allies can't help if they struggle to re-tell your story.
4. **Incorporate sound logic.** Flawed arguments risk any proposal's credibility.

The first three items – attention, memorability, virality – is about marketing. Logical proposals do not sell themselves.

I am a firm believer in David Ogilvy's famous quote: "When you have written your headline, you have spent 80 cents out of your dollar." Phrased differently, people care about how you *package* your ideas.

So, it doesn't matter if you're developing project names, product names, email subject lines, headlines, or just plain old text: make it count and make it zippy.

Use headlines

Give labels, headers, and names for ideas, descriptions, proposals, or other bodies of knowledge. I also call them headlines or signposts. It summarizes your main point, provides the reader where you're headed next, and gives readers an easy way to recall and reference ideas you've shared.

Use cliffhanger phrases

Steve Jobs knew the importance of suspense and drama. He'd pepper his presentations with phrases that would get audiences on the edge of their seats, eager to hear what Jobs had to say next. Learn those phrases.

Here are some of my favorites:

- *One more thing...*
- *Here's where it gets interesting...*
- *Here's where we're different...*
- *If you haven't been paying attention so far, you'll want to pay attention now because you don't want to miss this...*

My favorite zippy words

Lastly, to help inspire you, here's a list of my favorite zippy words:

Dreamy	Thrilling	Extraordinary
Exquisite	Vibrant	Remarkable
Delightful	Breathtaking	Unforgettable
Astonishing	Gorgeous	Must-have
Incredible	Irresistible	Unbeatable
Stunning	Life-changing	Inspiring
Surefire	Revolutionary	

3 Use the Rule of Three

The Rule of Three is a communication principle that suggests responses bundled in threes are more effective and satisfying. Put differently, the Rule of Three tells us to answer any "Why?" question with at least three reasons. Let's use a quick example:

YOU: *Why did you go to Stanford?*

ME: *I love the Bay Area.*

What do you think? Seems lacking, no? You might wonder, if I loved the Bay Area so much, why not UC Berkeley? Or Santa Clara University? The response would have been better if I provided two reasons instead of one. And three reasons would be significantly more thoughtful and compelling.

Steve Jobs loved the Rule of Three. When he introduced the iPod, he said, "Our competitors are no longer IBM, HP, and Dell. Our competitors are now Sony, Samsung, and LG." Or when he introduced the iPad, he said, "We have three major product families: the iPad, the iPhone, and the Mac." There's also a rhythmic quality. The Rule of Three is pleasing to the ear and easier to remember.

Challenge question: Can you find all the instances where I used the Rule of Three in this book?

4 Why You Need to Repeat Yourself

It's important to repeat your message again and again if you want to get your point across and influence others.

Thomas Smith's saying, while long and intended for product advertising, conveys elegantly why you need to repeat your message:

- The first time people look at any given ad, they don't even see it.
- The second time, they don't notice it.
- The third time, they are aware that it is there.
- The fourth time, they have a fleeting sense that they've seen it somewhere before.
- The fifth time, they actually read the ad.
- The sixth time they thumb their nose at it.
- The seventh time, they start to get a little irritated with it.
- The eighth time, they start to think, "Here's that confounded ad again."
- The ninth time, they start to wonder if they're missing out on something.
- The tenth time, they ask their friends and neighbors if they've tried it.
- The eleventh time, they wonder how the company is paying for all these ads.
- The twelfth time, they start to think that it must be a good product.
- The thirteenth time, they start to feel the product has value.
- The fourteenth time, they start to remember wanting a product exactly like this for a long time.
- The fifteenth time, they start to yearn for it because they can't afford to buy it.
- The sixteenth time, they accept the fact that they will buy it sometime in the future.
- The seventeenth time, they make a note to buy the product.
- The eighteenth time, they curse their poverty for not allowing them to buy this terrific product.
- The nineteenth time, they count their money very carefully.

- The twentieth time prospects see the ad, they buy what it is offering.

5 How to Be Authoritative Like a Professor

Use a whiteboard, as often as you can, to communicate your ideas. There are a couple of reasons why:

1. **Tailor your communication to your audience's learning style**. Some of us are audible learners; others are visual learners. Whiteboarding lets us accommodate both. You can also think of whiteboarding as doubling your communication bandwidth. Communicating both visually and audibly enhances your presentation.

2. **Be perceived as an authority figure**. There's something to be said about the power of the pen. Whiteboarders, standing at the front of the room, come across as professors. Listeners, sitting down, come across as students. The whiteboarder visually reinforces the perception that one is either an expert or an authority.

3. **Slow down your thinking**. Writing takes time, giving us extra cognitive cycles. Those cycles short circuit System 1 thinking and gives System 2 a chance to shine.

4. **Document**. Whiteboarding not only makes it easier for listeners to follow but also can be captured easily by smartphone.

6 Always Write Post-Meeting Notes

Why is it important to document what happened in general? There are a couple reasons why:

- **Personal record keeping**. Our memory is not perfect. Why not document with your favorite note-taking application, where the search function makes information easy to retrieve?
- **Gets everyone on the same page**. No more "he said, she said" uncertainty.
- **Makes those who weren't there feel included**. This includes remote attendees, your boss, or executives.
- **Showcase your leadership**. By sending notes to the team, you create visibility and show your value.

When should you write meeting notes?

I write meeting notes when there are:

- **Action items** that I don't want anyone to overlook.
- **Many attendees** at the meeting and I want to ensure we're all on the same page.
- **Critical decisions** being made, like an executive review meeting.
- **High stakes**, like a performance review.

I take notes as often as possible. The benefit far outweighs the time it takes to do so. If I'm busy, I'm willing to sacrifice detail and quality. Having some notes is infinitely better than not having anything at all.

When not to share meeting notes?

Sharing meeting notes would be odd and awkward at:
- Company-wide meetings
- Department trainings
- Meetings where notes have been distributed already or someone else indicated they would do so

How to do it?

In one-on-one meetings, anybody can write post-meeting notes. Simply email to the other person after the meeting, "Thanks for chatting with me. Here are my quick notes from our meeting."

In larger meetings, you can volunteer, or you can simply send it after the meeting, "Hi team, I wrote some key takeaways and action items from our group meeting. I'm passing it along in case you find helpful." Your initiative won't go unnoticed.

And don't forget speed matters: try to send the meeting notes the same or the next day at the latest. Their value degrades as the days and weeks go by. They are harder to draft too.

What should you include?

What you include is up to you. If you need ideas on format, you can search "meeting note templates" on Google. Here are some key areas I'd include in a meeting note:

- Takeaways
- Action items
- Date
- Attendees

Who do you share it with?

Send your meeting notes to all the attendees. Also include other stakeholders who might be interested, including your boss.

What's a better way of notetaking: typing or writing?

I always type meeting notes because they're easier to share via email.

For personal notes, I primarily use a paper journal. It's quick and fast. I also use an electronic note-taking application – either on my smartphone or laptop –when my journal is not available or when I want to save information that's easier to cut-and-paste like images and big paragraphs. Lastly, I love using graph pads when brainstorming designs, strategies, and other problem-solving activities. There's something about having a large, blank canvas when it comes to doing my best thinking.

7 Use Action Titles

Learn how to communicate effectively with PowerPoint. Most PowerPoint slides reflect the presenter's disorganized stream-of-consciousness.

Most slide titles describe what's on the slide. For example, "UPS Workforce Trends" is the title for this slide.

USPS Workforce Trends

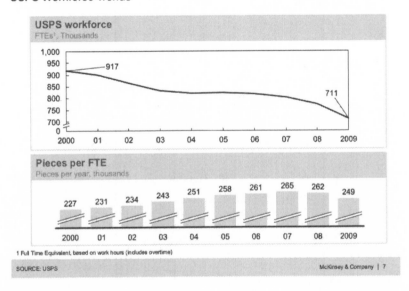

Although it's descriptive, the words "UPS Workforce Trends" is missing the main implications or takeaways of this slide.

The solution is to use action titles. An action title is a one-sentence summary that clarifies the slide's main takeaway. In other words, regular titles are more descriptive; action titles are more *explanatory*. Using action titles is the one thing you can do today to improve your PowerPoint skills.

Here's the same slide, but with a clear action title: "Recent reductions in workforce usage have been significant but pieces per FTE still declined in 2009."

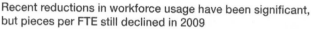

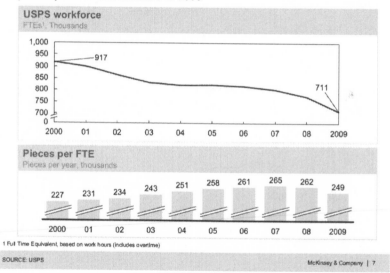

The slide title, in the form of a sentence, not only more completely describes what's on the slide, but also summarizes the main takeaway: pieces delivered per FTE has declined in 2009. Without the action title, it's less meaningful, memorable, and impactful.

Lastly, if you're looking for more tips, here are my favorite PowerPoint books:

- *Say it With Charts* by Gene Zelazny
- *Resonate* by Nancy Duarte

8 Beware of Analogies

Using analogies is common (but not necessary) among top communicators. However, using analogies is like telling jokes. People will remember if you do it well. Do it poorly, and you'll wish you didn't use analogies at all.

9 Remember the 5Ws and the H

The 5Ws and the H is a communication framework; it's a useful reminder of key questions your audience needs to comprehend a situation or evaluate your proposal.

For example, when understanding a new product, here is what listeners want to know:

- What is it?
- Who is it for?
- When is it ready?
- Where will it be available?
- Why should I get it?
- How does it work?

Challenge question: Did you catch all the instances where I used 5Ws and the H in the book?

10 How to Be a Good Storyteller

We can't resist a good story. Stories are better than an incoherent jumble, even if that jumble was adorned with charts and data.

Here's a reminder of what makes a good story:

Hero and villain

Every good story has a hero and a villain. In your stories, either you, your product or your company is the hero. The villain could be your competition, a rival, or gasp, an annoying boss or executive.

Characters

Share their actions, reactions, and motivations.

Dilemma

Discuss the central dilemma that needs to be resolved. Introduce tension.

Plot

Every good story has a beginning, middle, and end. Situation-complication-resolution is my favorite storytelling framework. The STAR method, situation-task-action-result, is another popular alternative.

Setting

Share details, such as place, time, people, and companies.

Don't forget to be specific! Corporate speak is dangerously vague and mysterious. Here's an example:

Marketing sucks.

A naïve bystander can unfairly conclude that the entire marketing department sucks upon hearing this vague, common one-liner.

Don't settle for this kind of sloppy communication. Instead, use names of people, places, and things. For instance, this statement, while longer, is clearer, more factual, and less likely to have varying interpretations:

William, from marketing, said we'd get 1,200 new sign-ups from the Celebrity Politician marketing campaign, but we only received 300. Since we missed our growth target, our lead investor bailed out of his follow-on commitment. I conclude, our marketing sucks.

11 Why Product Managers Need to Be Technical

Speak your audience's language. Doing so strengthens communication and shows respect, which leads us to a sensitive topic:

Do product managers need to be technical?

Yes.

Being technical will help you:

- **Communicate more effectively**, save time and minimize frustration for both you and your team members.
- **Be included more often** and get invitations to technical discussions.
- **Enhance credibility** and improve your odds of influencing others.
- **Better evaluate technical feasibility**, minimize wasted team effort, and suggest better solutions.

Non-techies and rusty techies may be dismayed by the need to be technical.

Can PMs survive without being technically proficient? Sure. Non-technical PMs can provide value elsewhere.

But the best concern themselves with technical details:

- Steve Jobs: Obsessed over chips on the Apple II motherboard
- Jeff Bezos: Delved into API details
- Elon Musk: Studied physics, rocket science, and energy development

Technical knowledge facilitates *sensible* moonshot visions and is key to persuading people to your vision.

12 Be Responsive, but Not Sloppy

Duncan Watts found that email response time is the single best predictor of whether one has a strong relationship with another.

This makes sense. We feel ignored, unvalued, and unappreciated when replies are missing or delayed. These days we expect teams to respond and reply throughout the day. At worst, reply within 24 hours.

Being unresponsive can be ruinous. I frequently see individuals become venomous because their counterparts failed to send notes in a timely manner.

Keep in mind that being responsive doesn't mean it's okay to be sloppy. Sloppy responses undo the benefit you've gained from being responsive. Instead, respond quickly with a note that is as factual and detailed as possible, given time and information constraints, and promise to follow up later.

CHAPTER 5

Skill 3: Tactical Awareness

Tactical awareness is the idea that small differences explain peak performance.

When most people zig, those with tactical awareness zag. Sometimes what they do is obvious; other times indiscernible.

When people say, you should work smarter, not harder – tactical awareness is that special magic that makes one more efficient at what they do.

Tactics

1 How to Establish Your Value

You may have heard about the "impostor syndrome" and its antidote, "fake it until you make it."

Both terms relate to one's self-worth. If you ever had the following thoughts, you're not alone:

- Do I belong?
- How does my boss (or peers) feel about my contribution?
- Am I the best (or even just good) at anything?
- My skills aren't valuable.
- How can I demonstrate value?
- When will I get promoted?

When you feel this way, here's what you should do:

Get ahead by getting started

It's hard to stop worrying. Meditate or talk to a therapist, if it helps. But as the Mark Twain saying goes, "The secret of getting ahead is getting started."

How to provide value

The next question is: what value should one provide? Related to this concept of value is the idea of specialization or developing a personal brand. You can specialize in a popular skill such as:

- **Technical**. Who doesn't want someone who can code? At the very least, it will build credibility with a cross-team of engineers.
- **Analytical**. Those who can write SQL queries or do Excel VLOOKUPs are always in high demand.
- **Design**. We all love someone who's a whiz with Sketch or Adobe Photoshop.
- **Storytelling**. It may not sound unique, but very few can tell a good story. Bonus points to those who can create McKinsey-like slides.

You can also choose trendy skills such as machine learning or augmented reality.

However, I feel obsessing over the "right" personal brand (or value to provide) is not only overblown but also a waste of time. You'll be surprised how many have gotten ahead with odd yet valuable skills:

- Ella Kinkead had a habit of reading every single email, in detail. This habit turned into a superpower. She was the team's personal Google; she could find any email in seconds. Her superpower made her a sought-after meeting participant. Ella's email habit allowed her to provide critical context others could not, leading to faster decision-making and shorter meetings. Ella is now a product VP at a Fortune 500 company.
- When executives asked questions, almost everyone complained about how the company didn't have the data or resources to answer. Robert Walters, however, was different. He took on those challenges and answered the executives' questions within a week. His can-do attitude made Robert a team favorite.

Expertise is one way to demonstrate worth and value. As you move up the career ladder, you'll find additional ways to demonstrate your worth and value including:

- **Conferring status** through promotions or awards.
- **Permitting access** to key stakeholders or information.
- **Granting resources** such as budget and headcount.

Lastly, this is not just for individuals only. A senior leader has a responsibility to demonstrate value, not just for herself, but for her team, especially if her team and charter is new.

2 How to Get Others to Do What You Want

We are driven primarily by our own personal interests. Other times we are driven by the interests of our boss, organization, or company. Either way, this is a great time to remind ourselves that others may not care about us or our objectives.

When influencing, always remember that effective influencers persuade by **framing their proposal or argument to the listener's interest.**

Here are some examples:

Listener's Goal	Your Frame
Desired to be promoted	"If your team works on our project, you'll present to the executives, which is two weeks before the next performance review."
Improve margins	"If you adopt this best practice, you'll reduce headcount by streamline DevOps."
Maintain a favorable environment	"The layoffs are coming. However, if you join the re-org committee, you can define the org structure and choose three new people to join your team."

When deducing one's personal motivations, I would:

- **Check their organizational goals.** Little wonder why the privacy & safety PM focuses on privacy and safety risks; it's their organizational goal.
- **Ask them or their confidants.** They might tell you how they like their liquor or how they feel about their spouse and family. You might be surprised what you can find out.

We can also deduce personal motivations using David McClelland's Need Theory. He found that 86 percent of the population can be categorized into one of these need states:

	Description	Appeal to their...
Achievement	These individuals like getting things done and love it when rewards are based on effort.	Desire for achievement by making them appear smart, enhancing their ego and reputation. You can also appeal to them by maintaining or building new reward systems or norms of value.
Affiliation	These individuals like relating to people, want to be included and seek affirmation from others.	People affinity by granting favors to their friends. They never want to put their allies in an uncomfortable spot.
Power	These individuals are competitive, love recognition, and influencing others.	Need for power by maintaining or increasing it.

If you struggle to deduce another's fears, hopes, beliefs or values, then do this instead: validate them. Everyone wants validation. So, hear them, see them, and make them feel what they say matters to you.[5]

---

[5] Inspired by Oprah Winfrey's quote from May 25, 2011

3 Ask for Stories, Not Opinions

With mentors, don't ask what to do. Ask what they did.

Many mentors have flawed opinions on how you can adapt their advice to your personal situation.

It's far safer for you to ask what they did. It'll inspire you and lead you to conclude, on your own, how their experience could apply to you.

4 Why it's Sometimes Good that Someone No-Shows or Otherwise Wrongs You

Most people get upset when someone is late or even worse, they get stood up for a meeting. But I have a different reaction when that happens. I'm thrilled.

Why? That person is going to feel bad, and they're going to make it up to me. Whatever future favor I've gained, it's usually a lot better than what I was supposed to get in the first place.

You'll be surprised the next time it happens to you. It works because of social norms: nobody wants to be remembered as a jerk. It also works because of reciprocity: we have the desire to be fair and not be indebted to others.

The only time this doesn't work is when:

1. **The other person is unaware that they've wronged you**. To remedy this, you can raise the issue, "I don't know if you realized this, but we had an appointment. And I traveled 45 minutes each way to be here today."
2. **The wrong is culturally accepted**. For example, Los Angeles traffic is notoriously bad. The residents often use traffic as an excuse for being late; as a result, few residents feel apologetic,

much less a need to right a wrong, when they are late. The person is truly cold-hearted.

5   *Go and See* for Yourself

Pioneered by Toyota, the "go see" problem-solving technique reminds us that by "go see" for ourselves we can more deeply understand the problem. We often do the opposite: we make the mistake of understanding issues through others.

Here are some examples of how you can "go see" in your day-to-day work.

Rather than...	Go see by...
Ask an engineer about the capabilities of a third-party API	Investigate and read about the third-party API on your own
Ask a customer or friend for a demo of a competitor's interface	Sign up for a free trial of the competitive product and walk through it yourself
Argue with in-house counsel about what's permissible under a partnership agreement	Ask for a copy of the contract and review yourself
Beg a designer to create a customer-facing image using Photoshop	Learn to create the image yourself using Microsoft PowerPoint

Adopt the "go see" method, and you'll be amazed how much better you'll:

- **Save time.**
- **Understand issues.**
- **Annoy coworkers less** by reducing the number of questions that you ask.

6 Ask the 5 Whys

Inspired by my wife, I've made a habit of asking "Why is that?" after most observations. This habit has helped me:

1. **Take notice.** Like many of you, I'm laser-focused on the next item on the to-do list; I rarely pause and ponder why. Why rob me of a chance to be intellectually curious?

2. **Expand my knowledge.** Asking why leads me to understand both the how and why of actions, events, and behaviors. Understanding why is required for any self-improvement fan.

Toyota arrived upon the same benefits of asking "Why?" Their innovation is called the "5 Whys," a problem-solving technique to determine the root cause of an issue. By asking "Why?" roughly five times, individuals will be closer to identifying the root cause of an issue.

Here's an example:

Why? Question	Answer
Why is the number of eCommerce conversions down week over week?	Because visits to the checkout page are down.
Why are checkout page visits down?	We released a new feature.
Why did we release a new feature?	We felt compelled to alert customers that we share their purchase data with third parties.
Why did we tell customers that we share their purchase data with third parties?	A new government regulation required that we do so.

| Why did the government regulation get passed? | Our partner was hacked two summers ago. During that hack, the government found out that we shared purchase data for 600 million customers with that partner. One year later, the government passed the new regulation. |

7 How to Be Constructive

If your company is like any engineering organization, your meetings are filled with this utterance: "Yes, that's a great idea, **but…**"

"Yes, but" is a false, insincere way of acknowledging someone's idea because the "but" shuts down the courageous innovator and silences further discussions. "Yes, but" is demoralizing and demotivating.

It impedes motivation. Why would anyone bother to suggest new ideas if they know others will attack, criticize, and mock their idea?

Given all the drawbacks, why do we keep using the "Yes, but" pattern? Some may say that we're being truthful: "The idea has flaws! Do you want me to lie and say, 'That's the best idea ever?'"

The "I'm telling the truth" line is a copout. The real reason we use "Yes, but" is because our ego and emotions get in the way. When a new idea surfaces, "Yes, but" lets us prove ourselves. Jealousy is another reason we use "Yes, but" – especially if we're unhappy that we're not in the spotlight.

Rather than demonstrate our self-worth at every opportunity, we must try to be vulnerable. Don't automatically shut down an idea. Who cares if you missed a chance to look smart?

Try "Yes, and..." instead

Feel what it's like to support your brave colleague who offered a unique thought or new proposal. Instead of reacting with a "Yes, but" respond to a colleague with a "Yes, and..." It reaffirms the original proposal, and it builds on top of the original suggestion, not undercut it.

You'll find you've encouraged and nurtured your colleagues to be more innovative, outspoken, and enterprising, but also allowed yourself to be vulnerable, and you'll find that you're not being perceived to be worth any less.

Turn Toward, not Away

Sometimes you don't have to use the words "Yes, but" to hurt relationships. Here's an example:

EMPLOYEE: *Last week, I went to our Colorado offices, and I learned several key insights from the engineering team we just acquired from XYZ Corp.*

BOSS: *Well, I went to the Paris, France offices last year, and I met with our former VP of Engineering. Here's what I learned from him...*

Did you catch what happened? The employee wanted to share, and the boss stole the spotlight. It's annoying and demoralizing. The boss also missed a chance to learn from the Colorado trip.

This is what researcher John Gottman calls "turning away." After studying successful relationships for decades, he found less successful partnerships "turn away" from each other whereas more successful partnerships "turn toward" each other. Those that turn away *reject* other parties' thoughts, concerns, and needs. And those that turn toward *addresses* them.

Gottman's "turn toward" philosophy is in-line with the "Yes, and…" technique; be sensitive to what your *rejection* behaviors do to your relationships *and* communication. Consider whether there's another way to voice your opinion without shutting down communication and rejecting others.

And one last reminder: interpersonal dynamics are key to winning allies, influencing others, and getting things done with large groups of people.

8   The One Question You Need to Ask

When a boss gives a new project, some reply with an obedient "okay." Others ask a never-ending train of What/Why/When questions.

However, Alex Sørensen used a different tactic. When receiving a new project, he'd ask his boss, "**How would you approach it?**"

Here's why his How question was remarkably clever: it invited Alex's boss to share her opinion. Grabbing a notepad, she'd diagram her approach for Alex.

Afterward, Alex clutched those notes like world-class recipes. After all, she outlined, step-by-step, what Alex needed to do.

Others would fumble the brand-new task through trial-and-error; Alex's results-driven boss did not have time for mistakes. Alex's clever How question allowed him to complete the task exactly the way she wanted it – quickly and efficiently.

We Need to Ask How Questions More Often

If we stopped to think about it, we rarely ask How questions. Why questions are the most common; it doesn't matter if we're young or old, we're always asking "Why?"

What/who/when questions are the next most prevalent. But how questions are so rare. Take your pick – a TV, the human voice, or a software feature – how often do we ask, "How does that work?"

Give How Questions a Chance

Imagine how you'd use How questions when talking to bosses, engineers, or your direct reports:

Rather than	Try this instead	Ideal when talking to
What do you want me to do?	How would you approach it?	Bosses
Why won't you build this feature?	How do you feel about this proposed feature from a scale of 1 to 10? (Follow-up) What would take it from a 6 to a 7 or even an 8?	Engineers
Can you draw a wireframe that...?	How would you draw a wireframe...?	Designers
Can you write a SQL query that...?	How would you write a SQL query that ...?	Data scientists and engineers
What did you do this week?	How are you feeling?	Direct reports

As you compare, you can see the benefits of How questions:

- **Not a command**. The alternative form is a command, request, or otherwise a burden on the other individual to do more work for you.
- **Strengthens relationships.** How questions reinforce relationships by inviting others to share their opinions or feelings.
- **Empowers**. If you learn how to do something for yourself, you've added to your arsenal of skills, making you more effective and valuable.

How Questions for Self-Improvement

One question we don't ask enough is, "How could I have done things differently?" whether it's after a meeting, presentation, or other critical interaction.

Instead of how questions, we typically ask questions that address our immediate emotions. For example, we appeal to our sense of fairness, when we ask, "*What* do I have to do to get a bigger salary?" Or we appeal to our need for validation, when we ask, "*Why* did I get recognized from my work on ___ project?"

One More Thing

Here's a clever tip from Bill White: after someone compliments your work, offer to show them *how* you did it. It's a clever way of incorporating the how question when your audience least expects it and increase your value at the same time.

9 Give Options

People like to be in control. So, if you want others to act, provide options. You're welcome to frame options in a way that nudges them to take the action you desire. If you don't provide choices, they can hesitate and choose to take no action at all.

10 Be a Thought Leader

Strive to be a thought or opinion leader. Thought leaders carry importance including status, unique expertise, authority, or say that comes from being an opinion leader.

Being a thought leader makes a difference in your day-to-day. It'll also standout favorably during promotion time.

11 Use the Wisdom of the Crowd

Your personal point of view may not be representative of the group. Polling others can be as easy as grabbing three or four people for a quick opinion.

12 The Power of Observation

Bosses have an endless list of problems. They'd gladly have you take problems off their hands.

There are many ways to eliminate problems. Proposing a solution can be one step in the right direction.

However, high performers understand something that others do not. That is, if you want to increase your chances of:

- Looking good, then focus on observing and identifying problems.
- Looking bad, then focus on giving solutions.

How can this be? First, all of us are blessed with the incredible power of observation, regardless of our expertise. For instance, your parents may not be communication experts, but if they believe your presentation is boring, it probably is. Granted, some observers are more astute. But it doesn't make their observations any less correct.

On the flip side, our power to conjure the *perfect* solution is terrible. The probability of a solution being 100% perfect is very low, regardless of who gives it. Solutions require a long list of considerations including timing, creativity, relevancy, objectives, constraints, and execution. Coming up with the perfect solution is like solving a multivariate equation whereas a perfect observation is like solving a single variable equation.

If you're still skeptical, then do one last test: would you be more successful in identifying problems or coming up with solutions to your country's health care system?

Moving on, we can deduce the following:

1. **Coach others to coach you**. Use other people's power of observation to help you. They do not have to be experts. For example, even novices can point out problem behaviors such as:
    a. The number of "ahs" and "ums" in your speech.
    b. Moments that trigger your self-deprecating behavior.
    c. Phrases that ignite your stress behaviors.
2. **Do not let your coaching ability breed overconfidence**. Bosses, mentors, and executives alike fall in love with the sound of their own voice. Stay humble and be gentle. It's always easier observed than solved.
3. **Burnish your personal reputation**. When voicing your opinions, it's safer to share observations than solutions.

One more thing, am I advocating that you should avoid proposing solutions at all? No. If your job necessitates solutions then do so. My main point is this: aside from leveraging the power of observation as much as possible, if you're at a company where it's *favorable or necessary to maintain a good image*, I'd focus on observing problems than proposing solutions.

13 Rubber Ducking

"Rubber duck debugging" is a way of finding and fixing errors from computer software or hardware. By explaining the error or situation to another, the programmer often figures out the answer, on their own.

Later, the programmer realizes that the listener played a minor, if any, role when arriving at the solution. Thus, we joke that many programmers can solve their problems by talking to a rubber duck.

I love rubber duck debugging. Here's why:

Empowers us

We build confidence knowing that we can solve our own problems.

Maintains individual responsibility

The best person to solve a problem is the person who knows it best: the individual working on it. We shouldn't attempt to pass our problems to someone else.

Reduces meddling

Rubber ducking reminds our bosses that they are unlikely to have the best solution because they aren't intimate with the details. It also reminds us that the best thing a boss can do is listen.

Serves as a codeword for empathy

With my colleagues, I trigger rubber duck debugging by saying, "Cecile, I want to rub*ber duck* something with you..." or "Donna, why don't you *quack it out* with Ana..." I do this because I want to:

1. Warn them that I'm about to start a potentially incoherent jumble of ideas and arguments.
2. Start their listening skills.
3. Most importantly, trigger their support and suspend their judgment.

The third one is particularly important. I shouldn't be judged or punished when asking for help.

It takes courage to admit that I don't have an answer, share an unpolished stream-of-consciousness, or admit to talking to toys.

One last thing: the listener can help facilitate or trigger rubber ducking with a well-placed question here or there. Here are some of my favorites:

Facilitation questions
- So, what's going on?
- What have you tried? And why didn't that work?
- And of course, the 5 Whys.

Brainstorming
- Have you considered _____?
- How did <similar product X> solve that problem?
- Who's good at solving _____? And how would they approach this problem?

- When was the last time you solved a similar problem? And how did you resolve that situation?

14 The Truth about Mentors

Your typical mentoring relationship

Almost all mentoring relationships are one-sided: the mentee asks for advice and the mentor answers. In the best case, the mentee gains valuable insights. In the worst case, the mentee merely glorifies the mentor's ego. Since mentors are often unfamiliar with the mentee's day-to-day work, mentors dispense generic and usually irrelevant advice.

Although the mentor gets the mentee's admiration, the mentor can get frustrated too. When the mentee discards the relationship, the mentor can feel used

When people say, "I want a mentor," what they really want is a *sponsor*. The terms mentor and sponsor are often confused.

Sponsors and protégés

Having a sponsor is different. The sponsor and protégé relationship is a bilateral, mutually beneficial relationship. First, they are well-aware of each other's work because they work in the same company *and* organization.

The sponsor needs junior employees to achieve their objectives. Maybe the sponsor needs technical skills. Or perhaps they need a protégé to dutifully finish whatever that is sent his way.

In return, the sponsor rewards the protégé with promotions and political air cover. And because the protégé holds a special place in the sponsor's heart, the sponsor is eager to mentor and counsel the protégé.

The relationship endures because the sponsor and protégé need one another.

Qualifications of a sponsor

It's easier to get promoted if your sponsor has influence and organizational control. Sponsors are rarely your immediate manager. Here are a few reasons why:

1. Your immediate manager may not have enough control or openings to accelerate your career.
2. Your immediate manager isn't incentivized to promote you to be her peer. At best, the manager will have to replace your missing productivity. At worst, the manager just promoted you to be her new rival.

In the rare situation where your immediate manager has enough influence and is not threatened by your rise, that person could be your sponsor.

How does one find a sponsor?

*   **Sponsors are likely to be in your chain of command.** It is odd for sponsors to assign projects and promote a protégé that's not within their organization.
*   **Sponsors typically select you, not the other way around.** Sponsors have their eye out for capable individuals who can take on special projects. Sponsors do not choose unremarkable performers. Find opportunities to shine and demonstrate your worth.
*   **When you get your shot, don't pass it up.** Sponsors are looking for protégés more often than you think. Sponsors are ambitious, and they need help. Many protégé candidates

unknowingly pass, unaware of the mutually beneficial relationship that could occur.

One last thing: is a sponsor and protégé relationship declared publicly? No. A sponsor and protégé relationship will never be formally proposed or documented. It'll start casually and small, like a request to help with an important project. When you've been summoned, don't hesitate. Plunge in and give the sponsor a chance. From there, the typical sponsor and protégé pair implicitly understand what each one needs to do and what they'll get out of it.

15 Data-driven decision-making is good. But intuitive decision-making is not bad either.

Analysis and intuition are both important. And both have drawbacks.

Those with an analytical decision-making style are more accurate but slow. They need to learn to analyze and make decisions more quickly. Those with an intuitive decision-making style are fast but error-prone. They need to learn to make decisions more accurately.

This relates to a larger point. Nothing is ever 100 percent good; there are always drawbacks. And nothing is ever 100 percent bad. There's always a silver lining.

Moderation is key. Strive to build a balanced skill set and emotions. It will help you weather both good times and bad.

16 Minimize Your Work Inventory

Product development is highly perishable; assumptions about technologies and the market can quickly become obsolete.

Any lean startup devotee would not find this surprising. But most would assume that lean startup means eliminating waste. For instance, refrain from coding if you get the same learnings with an inexpensive paper prototype.

But I'm asking you to take it further: keep your product backlog lean. There's no need for five-year, one-year, or possibly six-month product roadmaps. Given the pace of technology, what felt crucial a few weeks ago, may not be important now.

So, in addition to not wasting time writing requirements for features five years from now, if you're not sure whether you should build a feature, just wait. You might find out in a couple of weeks that the world may have changed. The feature that you thought would solve your problem...well, perhaps the solution is no longer possible, or the problem is no longer there.

And please, don't confuse this advice with doing away with a product vision. Those need to be intact and committed to for at least 10 years.

17 Show and Tell Your Work

In our daily stand-up meeting, my designer Mia has established a routine of showing her work. By doing so, she's employed the same principles that allow Kanban boards to work so well: both Mia and the Kanban boards visualize work in progress. Doing so increases coordination visibility and minimizes requests for information.

Weekly reports, daily updates, newsletters, and status meetings provide transparency too.

In addition to reducing time, effort, and uncertainty from your teammates, providing visibility into your work will burnish your reputation too, which will be handy during promotion time.

One last note: showing your work is even more critical if you, or other team members, are based in remote offices.

18 The Ladder of Knowledge

Sam Altman once said, "Not knowing something shouldn't be an excuse for not getting things done." He believed that anyone could "learn almost anything."

Following Altman's lead, we can declare that knowledge enables action. As a result, you'll need to know 1) when you've acquired enough knowledge to do your job well and 2) whose knowledge to count on when making decisions. Use the following four-step framework to help you assess your own and others' knowledge levels.

Step 1: Familiarity

This is the knowledge that you remember from a college course 10 years ago. Or it could be a 15-minute Wikipedia article that you just read on a new, unfamiliar topic.

The jargon feels familiar, but you don't feel comfortable applying that knowledge.

The most brazen believe their Step 1 knowledge is enough; you can spot them as those who dismiss guest speakers with a dismissive "I've heard that before."

Step 2: Understanding

Those with Step 2 understanding participate in meetings and can follow the conversation. From time-to-time, they ask meaningful questions or commentary. But Step 2s rely on experts to tell them what's doable and what's not. Step 2s might have a sense that something is off, but they can't articulate why something is off or how it should be.

Most managers have Step 2 understanding of their team's day-to-day work. When Step 2s say, "I know enough to be dangerous" that means they understand basic concepts, but if they demonstrate too much confidence in their knowledge, they'll make mistakes and miss important details.

Finally, those with Step 2 understanding are unlikely to teach a course on the topic, because they haven't had enough practical experience, with nuances of the subject, to answer moderately difficult questions.

Step 3: Application

Step 3s have extensive hands-on experience. They've done it repeatedly. They've found ways of making it better; they've found ways of making it worse. They can articulate the pros and cons of different implementation methods.

Others may wrongly believe that Step3s are experts, due to their knowledge in a small yet incomplete number of topics.

Step 4: Mastery

It's easy to spot Step 4s. Their mastery is so strong that they've taught others the subject matter, perhaps for a decade or more. There's no teaching challenge they can't handle. Masters never use their poor communication skills as an excuse. They can teach the hopeless to become masters too; they will never write-off learners as incapable.

19 How to Know if You're Done, if You've Never Done It Before

Let's say you're striving for step 4 knowledge. Or maybe you want to create a deliverable or result that feels like a step 4 master created it. How do you know when you've reached that point? The real answer is probably never. There's always new knowledge or insights to acquire. Or the final deliverable could always be better. But that's not 100 percent practical. We can't spend forever working on something.

So instead you might want to try the Navy's 40 percent rule. That is, when you think you're done, you're only 40 percent complete.

The 40 percent rule is a check on our overconfidence. Just when we've told ourselves that there's nothing more to be done, improved, or even learned – the 40 percent rule reminds us we still have 60 percent to go.

20 How to Learn a New Task or Subject

Today's changing work environment means you'll have to learn all the time.

When learning something new, a web search for templates, checklists, and how-to guides can be a good start. But what if your area doesn't have templates or how-to guides?

In that case, construct your own how-to guide and teach yourself. There's no better way to learn than the four-step method I'll call the IDPS Method™:

- **Identify**. Who are the best thought leaders in the space?
- **Decompose**. Which topics should you know?
- **Prioritize**. Which topics will give you the biggest benefit?
- **Sequence**. What order should you learn the topics?

Identify the Experts

Don't reinvent the wheel. Instead, to learn quickly, stand on the shoulders of experts.

Here are a few questions you can use to identify top thought leaders, in any domain:

- Who are the top three thought leaders in the space?
- What are the top three books that industry experts have on their bookshelf?
- What are the best instructional books on this subject?

For a bigger edge, utilize these questions to discern lesser-known experts:

- Who are the most impressive, lesser-known teachers?
- What are the most impressive, lesser-known books in the space?

Decompose & Prioritize

It can be intimidating to learn everything at once. Use these questions to determine what to focus on first:

- If I could only do three things to get better in this area, what would that be?
- If I had only 24 hours to prepare for a competition where I must perform _____ to win $5,000,000, what _____ things should I do?

Sequence

Next, when determining an appropriate sequence, factor in:

- **Importance**. Why learn something if it's not relevant or useful to you?
- **Pre-requisites**. Why study an advanced topic when you haven't studied the prerequisites yet?

- **Frustration minimization.** Is there a logical progression to learning the material? Is it more effective, for you, to tackle the easier items first? Or vice versa?
- **Rewards.** Do you need a reward for motivation?

Lastly, here's a set of questions to figure out what not to learn or do:

- First, what are the biggest mistakes novices make when learning X? What are the biggest misuses of time?
- At the pro level, what mistakes are most common?

Individual Awareness

21 Don't Just Focus, but Obsess

It's not enough to simply focus or do less.

What you choose to focus on, you must obsess. It's from that obsession that leads to great results.

22 How to Search for Personal Weaknesses

It goes without saying: the fewer weaknesses one has, the more one can do.

This leads to the next question: how do you determine your weaknesses? Fortunately, there's no need to purchase an expensive personality test. Chances are you have the answers already.

Ask yourself

What triggers an emotional reaction? Exploring negative emotions is an effective way to identify weaknesses.

Do you...

- Get *nervous* in front of people? If so, you may have social anxiety.
- *Regret* making decisions? If so, you may have a fear of failure.
- *Worry* that others may not be impressed by your job title? You may have a low sense of self-worth.

Ask your significant other

He or she spends a big chunk of time with you. They probably have seen you at your worst. What they say is your weakness likely has some truth behind it.

Ask your family

Siblings work well because they don't hold anything back. If they say you're entitled or selfish, they are probably right.

Parents can work too, but they're often blinded by unconditional love. Whatever your flaws may be, parents often deny and instead think you're the best.

You can try your boss, co-workers, and friends. They're like your parents: you'll have to review their feedback critically. On the one hand, co-workers and friends may have useful, first-hand observations. On the other hand, they may have reasons for not sharing everything you need to know.

23 Common Biases

Humans are irrational, and our cognitive biases often explain our cloudy judgment.

Wikipedia lists 185 cognitive biases. IARPA, a US government agency, deemed these six biases to be the most important, which I'll discuss in more detail:

1. Confirmation Bias
2. Fundamental Attribution Error
3. Dunning-Kreuger Effect
4. Anchoring Effect
5. Representative Heuristic
6. Projection Bias

Confirmation Bias

Confirmation bias is considered the most pervasive and damaging bias of them all; we tend to search and favor information that confirms our own beliefs.

For example, if we prefer fast decision-making styles, we're less likely to consider slow decision-making styles.

Exploiting Confirmation Bias

Exploit confirmation bias as a social skill. For instance, gain favor with another by sharing views that are in-line with an acquaintance's beliefs.

Countering Confirmation Bias

Counter confirmation bias by seeking information that disproves our beliefs. Wargaming or playing devil's advocate is another way to question deeply held beliefs.

Fundamental Attribution Error

Fundamental attribution error states the following:

	Fundamental attribution error predicts that we...
When receiving good news...	Emphasize personal reasons and de-emphasize external reasons for the good news
When receiving bad news...	Emphasize external reasons and de-emphasize personal reasons for the bad news

For example, if we receive a bad performance review, we tend to blame our boss or an unforgiving bell curve (systemic reasons) rather than hold ourselves accountable (personal reasons).

However, if we receive a good performance review, we conversely attribute the good review to our performance rather than credit a favorable relationship with our boss or the company's generous review system.

Exploiting Fundamental Attribution Error

Exploit the fundamental attribution error by associating our careers with name-brand companies, well-regarded leaders, and highly sought-after projects. Future talent managers, spellbound by the fundamental attribution error, may incorrectly ascribe your success to your individual ability rather than your good fortune in latching onto the right companies, projects, and individuals.

Countering Fundamental Attribution Error

Counter the fundamental attribution error through awareness. For instance, we can closely examine how a candidate's situation – that is factors outside of their control – affected his or her successes to date.

Bias Blind Spot

The bias blind spot is based on the belief that one is less biased than a normal person. A related concept is the Dunning-Kruger effect where low-skilled individuals mistakenly believe their abilities are greater than they are. Both concepts relate to one's motivation to perceive themselves positively.

For instance, in a survey of 600 people, 85 percent said they were less biased than the average person. Clearly, there is bias here. If the respondents were not susceptible to the bias blind spot, we would expect 50 percent of respondents to say they were less biased.

Exploiting the Bias Blind Spot

Exploit the Dunning-Kruger effect and bias blind spot by exploiting an adversary's overconfidence. For example, bait adversaries to take projects they mistakenly believe they would succeed in, only to see them fail.

Countering the Bias Blind Spot

Counter the bias blind spot by slowing down our thinking, pushing ourselves to get a broader or larger set of opinions, and considering the pros and cons of our beliefs more deeply.

Anchoring Effect

The anchoring effect is when we rely on an initial piece of information when making estimates. Biased by that initial piece of information, we make insufficient adjustments from the original.

For example, if we previously built a feature in six months, we assume that building a similar feature would take six months too. However, another team, unbiased by the six-month data point, may conclude the feature would only take one week, using modern techniques.

Exploiting the Anchoring Effect

Exploit the anchoring effect by offering to write the first draft of a roadmap, presentation, or document. Anchored by the content in the first draft, you'll increase your chance of getting what you want.

Countering the Anchoring Effect

Counter the anchoring effect by ignoring the information anchor. Returning to the two previous examples, I would ignore the six-month historical precedent or suggest to re-write a document from scratch.

Representative Heuristic

Representative heuristic refers to when we wrongly judge something to be more likely because it's more representative.

An example is the famous Linda experiment. The experiment described a fictional woman Linda who appeared to be a feminist: committed to social justice, majored in philosophy, and participated in antinuclear demonstrations. Researchers then asked the subjects which was more likely: a) Linda was a bank teller or b) Linda was a bank teller and feminist. More than 80 percent of subjects chose b).

Statistics experts know that b) cannot be more likely than a). It's less probable that one would meet the bank teller *and* feminist condition (i.e. conjunction of the two sets).

Exploiting the Representative Heuristic

Many executives exploit the representative heuristic when making big investments. If other companies with similar strengths and capabilities can succeed, why wouldn't we succeed as well?

Countering the Representative Heuristic

Counter the representative heuristic by focusing on prior probabilities, also known as base rates.

Projection Bias

Projection bias is when one overestimates the present when determining preferences in the future.

For example, a company that does business primarily in the United States may underestimate their likelihood of doing business *outside* the United States in the future.

Exploiting Projection Bias

Exploit projection bias by agreeing to unfavorable terms, with a strong inkling that those same terms are favorable under *future* conditions.

Countering Projection Bias

Counter the projection bias by thinking about how the future would appear.

Three More to Consider

Aside from the six biases suggested by IARPA, here are three more that you should be familiar with as a PM:

Survivorship bias

Making false conclusions based on sampling error. For example, product managers often make conclusions about what makes a successful product without considering unsuccessful products, which are less likely to be top of mind.

Negativity bias

Negativity bias is a cognitive error where negative consequences have a greater effect than positive consequences. For example, homeowners are more obsessed with preventing the loss of their home rather than reducing their insurance payments.

Stereotyping

There are many stereotypes, but the one I'd like you to consider is attractiveness stereotyping. That is, gorgeous products are assumed to have desirable characteristics (e.g. fun, professional, more expensive, or high market share) vs. products that are ugly.

Emotional Awareness

24 Use Therapy for the Past; Meditation for the Future

Sometimes, we ruminate about the past. Other times, we worry about the future.

To stop ruminating, go to therapy.

To stop anxiety, mediate.

Live in the present, and you will find contentment.

25 How to Meditate

The word, meditate, has many definitions including:

1. Think deeply or carefully about something
2. Focus one's mind for a period, in silence, as a method of relaxation

When I say "meditate," I'm referring to the second definition.

Why should you meditate?

Our heads have a lot of chatter; we often worry about the future like a big deadline or an uncertain event (e.g. results of a company-wide re-organization).

Worry is unproductive. In fact, it's usually debilitating. Ease your mind from anxiety by learning how to meditate.

How do you meditate?

After you close your eyes and begin to breathe, these are the three key steps:

1. **Be present**. Acknowledge the sounds, smells, and if your eyes are open, what you see.
2. **Notice when your mind starts to wander**. Your thoughts might float to the future or ruminate about the past. That's okay. Minds tend to wander. Don't chastise yourself.
3. **Let your mind go back to focusing on the present**.

If meditation is new to you, meditating for five minutes might be difficult. Who can sit still for five minutes, right? To remedy the problem, try chanting. It can keep your mind from wandering. Repeat a multi-syllable word like "Mi-cro-soft" to maintain your focus on the present.

However, with more practice (focusing on just these three steps), you'll meditate longer and reap the reward of a clearer mind as well as a head and heart free from anxiety.

Why doesn't meditation work for ruminations about the past?

As humans, we seek meaning. Suppressing ruminations about the past may work for you but generally, I find it less effective than simply making meaning. Once you've made meaning of the past, you'll find it easier to move on.

Rather than meditating, isn't it better to get things done?

If you're facing a simple task, a minute doing may be better than five minutes meditating. Or for more daunting tasks, an hour planning may be more effective than doing or an hour's worth of meditation.

26 How to Keep an Emotional Journal

We ruminate because we try to make meaning of our world. When the world makes sense (and when we make sense of ourselves) we are fulfilled. However, making sense of what is happening or what has happened is hard to do on our own.

We could all use a professional therapist to help us make sense of the past. The lucky few have a confidant. For some, that confidant is a spouse who's skilled at making sense of the past and soothing those unnecessary and debilitating ruminations.

Be careful about using unwilling spouses and friends as your therapist. Therapy is hard work, and it's not fair to monopolize their time and hold them responsible for fixing your mental baggage.

You can always try self-therapy by journaling your thoughts. Journaling gets ruminations out of your head and onto paper. Journaling will help make sense of your thoughts, refreshing you in the process.

It can be hard to journal without prompts. My favorite journaling prompts come from Tony Schwartz:

Question	Example
What specifically triggers you?	My boss said he doesn't want me to spend time with my family.
How does that make you feel?	Hurt. Not accepted. Trapped. I don't know how I can meet my obligations to my company and my family.
How do you typically act?	I make snide remarks. Like today I told Elena only the dull and

	stupid spend more than 40 hrs. in the office.
What is the impact on you and others?	Feels like my boss is making me choose between my family and work.
	It's not fair for me to work long hours when friends get easy jobs and high salaries.
What part of what happened is a fact?	He sent a Tweet that said, "There are way easier places to work, but nobody ever changed the world on 40 hours a week."
What is the story you told?	My boss doesn't want me to spend time with my family.
What was the effect of your response?	Resent my boss.
How would you tell the story by looking at the big picture rather than focusing on the immediate threat to your value?	My boss wants our company to do great things and change the world.
How would you tell the story from the perspective of the person who triggered you?	Our work is not supposed to be easy. We can't treat our jobs as a regular 40-hour job if we're going to change the world.
How would you tell the story from the perspective of how you can grow and learn from the experience over time?	My boss wants me to do great things, so I shouldn't expect to coast at work. He's not saying I can't spend time with my family, but I will have to prioritize how I spend time at and outside of

> work. And I should be less stingy about working a few extra hours here and there.

Finally, how often should you journal? Some choose to journal either at the start or end of the day. I choose to journal when I feel I need to.

27 Learn How to Forgive

Forgive the flaws of others. Like you, they're human. They make mistakes, and you'll feel better if you treat them with compassion.

And while you're at it, learn to forgive yourself. We are often our worst critics.

Interpersonal Awareness

28 How to Avoid Rivalries

Others will imitate you if you do something worthy. Get comfortable with those who copy your work, steal your projects, and become your rivals.

Do note that sometimes we *unwittingly* create rivals by rejecting someone or treating them unfairly. When this happens, your rivals will compete harder. They want to savor your defeat. And they will seek a way to harm, hurt, and otherwise seek vengeance. Be gracious.

29 Always Check the Emotional Temperature

How many times have your peers said, "Okay," but not everything is okay?

That's right. Many utterances have an emotional undercurrent. Feelings matter; dig deep to understand and then address others' emotions.

To effectively deal with others' emotions, use this three-step process:

Label their feelings

Labeling their feelings is a way to make others feel heard and understood. Many folks are opaque about how they truly feel. Sometimes they're trying to maintain a professional poker face. Other times, they can't verbalize how they feel aside from the fact that they're "not feeling good."

Thus, you'll have to work to uncover the true feelings and concerns. Here are some phrases to help you understand others:

Denial Phrases

Example 1

THEM: *That isn't the case.*

YOU: *I get the sense that you think I disagree. Why?*

Other Denial Examples

I don't think that's fair.

No one else thinks that.

Sham Acceptance or Other Passive-Aggressive Behavior

Example 1

YOU: *Can you implement feature X by Friday?*

THEM: *Ok.*

YOU: *Even though you're saying yes, I don't get the sense you're happy.*

Example 2

YOU: *On a scale of 1 to 10, how do you feel about this?*

THEM: *A three.*

YOU: *Why so low? And what would move it from a three to an eight?*

Other Sham Acceptance Examples

I hear you.

Thank you, bye.

OK then, fine.

Mistrust

THEM: *You've always wanted me to screw up.*

YOU: *You feel I'm wishing for your failure.*

THEM: *Yes.*

YOU: *What makes you think that?*

Other Mistrust Examples

Is this because you want to fire me? I always thought you were selfish. So...why are you doing this?

Share your story

After the other party has had a chance to share their story and feel understood, assess whether it's safe to share your story. If it is, share your story not only in a manner that provides context and facts, but also to demonstrate that you harbor no mal-intent or hidden agendas. Here's an example:

THEM: *When I asked for your help during the conference call, you gave a flat "no."*

YOU: *I was distracted when I was cold-called during the meeting. I was typing an email and trying to meet a deadline.*

Figure a way forward

Lastly, figure out a way forward. It could be a combination of an apology, compromise, or a plan to prevent the unfortunate occurrence from happening again. Here's an example:

THEM: *That wasn't nice.*

YOU: *You're right. I was wrong to shut you down so abruptly. I'm sorry. I'll promise to be more thoughtful when I answer questions rather than simply reacting. I'll also make a note to not multitask during meetings so that I give everyone my full attention.*

30 Don't Be Passive-Aggressive

Here's why:

- **Your co-workers can't read your mind**. They're even more unlikely to decipher your nuanced suggestions when they're stressed or busy.

- **It's a futile way of solving problems or venting frustration**. You're unlikely to get a solution. Even acknowledgment might be a stretch.

- **It damages relationships**. Passive-aggressive communicators use innuendo and deception, which builds suspicion.

- **Being clear, assertive, and direct isn't as bad as it seems**. We resort to passive-aggressive communication because we fear confrontation, rejection, and dealing with the other person's reaction. You can be assertive without coming across as unkind, insulting, offensive, or confrontational.

Many of us who are passive-aggressive don't know that we are. But you can detect this with one simple question. Ask your peers, "Do I communicate in a clear, open, assertive, and straightforward way?" If there's hesitation (i.e. anything less than an unequivocal yes) then you have some work to do.

31 Have Lunch with Everyone

A clever tactic is to have lunch with everyone in your company or if it's more reasonable, your department or division. It'll force you to meet more people, build relationships, and gain new information.

And do it as a 1:1, not group, lunch. 1:1 lunches forger closer and more substantial connections.

Speaking of close connections, push yourself to be the first person to have lunch with new employees. Many new employees don't have lunch plans on the first day or week at work. They'll be touched that you reached out to them first, and you'll win a special place in their heart.

32 Resolve Conflict with Your Bosses

If your boss' priorities conflict with priorities from her leadership chain, help her. Nudge your boss to align with your skip. You may feel that it is not your place to raise the issue; however, any conflict between your immediate boss and your skip will make you miserable. You'll feel confused, rudderless, and worst of all, extremely anxious. Raise the issue because it will help you and your boss.

Here's some sample wording to help kickstart that conversation:

YOU: *I have a sensitive issue to raise.*

BOSS: *Go ahead. What's on your mind?*

YOU: *I feel I'm getting mixed signals from you and your boss.*

BOSS: *How so?*

YOU: *Your boss wants me to move fast and break things. But you want me to be thoughtful and not impulsive.*

BOSS: *Why can't you do both?*

YOU: *If I move fast, I may not have time to think of all the different use cases. If I'm more deliberate, we'll end up shipping less often. I feel like if I please one person, I'll just disappoint the other. And I'm concerned this will affect my upcoming performance review.*

BOSS: *Got it. Let me talk to her, and I'll clarify how we'd like you to proceed going forward.*

CHAPTER 6

Skill 4: Extraordinary Mental Toughness

Extraordinary mental toughness is superhuman willpower that allows exceptional PMs to persevere over trying moments.

1 Be the Last to Quit

True PM legends invent billion-dollar businesses from scratch or lead expansion into 100 new countries.

Google's Sundar Pichai is an example of a PM legend. Google, in its early years, famously proclaimed that it would never build a web browser or desktop operating system. But Pichai pushed and willed the Chrome browser and the Chrome OS into existence.

Pichai's insistence was rewarded. Despite a saturated browser market, Pichai turned the Chrome browser into the world's number one browser, beating incumbent browsers from Apple, Microsoft, and Mozilla.

Here's the difference between heroes – like Pichai – and everyone else: they're the last to quit.

The excuses and lies we tell ourselves allow us to quit more often than we'd like to admit. How often have you heard the excuses below?

- *I don't need to be technical.*
- *I don't need to work for a name brand company.*
- *I'm not the kind of person to go for big promotions or titles.*
- *Why should we build a browser when the market is saturated and dominated by strong competition? We can do better things with our time and money.*

When we buy into these excuses, we give up. When we give up, we can't win because we're not on the court.

Conversely, many individuals win simply because they're the only ones left. This is what people mean when they say 90 percent of life is showing up.

2 Disagree and Then Commit

At first, I thought this phrase meant each person's job is to disagree and not waver. In other words, have conviction.

Conviction is important, but this phrase means something different altogether.

Disagree

Coined by Amazon, "Disagree and then commit" means that you have a right — perhaps even an obligation — to *disagree* with a proposal, opinion, or course of action.

Conventional wisdom tells us that good leaders build consensus. That advice is incomplete and misleading.

Great leaders, when making decisions, seek out as many dissenting opinions as possible.

Dissensions multiply options, deepen one's understanding of a problem, and stir the imagination. Leaders who focus only on building consensus, at the expense of seeking dissension, may thoughtlessly obey recommendations from their lieutenants.

Then Commit

The second half is equally important. After voicing a dissenting point view, one shouldn't stubbornly cling to it, especially if the company or group decides otherwise. Instead, the dissenter should commit to the group's agreed-upon goal or action. Committing keeps a group focused on the same objective. As the popular saying goes, "A house divided cannot stand."

3 How to Tolerate Stress

In a corporate environment, few things induce more stress than a big presentation.

When it comes to managing stress, I'm not going to propose that you go to the gym, try breathing exercises, spend more time with friends, or any other techniques you'll find online. While they can help, I do not believe they are the most effective. Here's why:

We get stressed because we want to do well. Our ego is on the line. The consequences are high. For many, an executive presentation is a rare opportunity to demonstrate our worth to executives and your boss' peers. Your performance can impact your next promotion.

We also stress because we don't know:

- **How the audience will react**
- **What to say** both during the presentation or impromptu questions afterward

However, if we really thought about it, we could anticipate 90 to 95 percent of the questions they're going to ask. At the very least, the 5Ws and the H should not surprise us at all.

Knowing this, we should prepare by writing out what we're going to say during the presentation. We should also jot answers to their anticipated questions.

And it's not enough to just write. We need verbal rehearsal as well. And ask a friend to mimic audience behaviors like being critical or silent.

The best speakers rehearse dozens of times. Eleanor Roosevelt, an experienced public speaker, was known to rehearse more than 100 times for important speeches. It's no surprise that Roosevelt got exceptional results.

4   Watch Out for Errors of Omission

Lying is rare.

When we lie, we feel guilt. We also fear the consequences of lying. Lastly, keeping different stories in our heads is mentally taxing too.

Instead, we and our co-workers do something else: leave information out. We're irreproachable because a breezy "I would've told you if you asked" gets us off the hook!

As a leader, your job is to figure out what is left out. Unfortunately, that's hard. For example, if we see a group of apples and then an orange, we can quickly spot what doesn't belong. The orange.

However, if we were to think about what should be included (in other words, the omission) it's harder to solve. Perhaps we need to include:

- *More oranges*?
- *Other fruits*, like a banana, blueberry, or strawberry?
- *Cocktail supplies* like a blender, glass, and a splash of liquor?

The possibilities are endless. All seemingly probable. Here are some tips on how to better spot omissions:

Increase your domain expertise

The more you know, the less you'll miss. Hire an expert if you don't have time to learn.

Brainstorm alternate explanations

Is the man on the street yelling at you because he's rude? Mentally unstable? Or is he telling you that you're going the wrong way on a one-way street?

Strengthen your intuition

Peter Drucker encouraged executives to record their estimates like a profit or production goal. Then he wanted executives to compare their estimates with the actual as a means of strengthening their intuition.

Use checklists & templates as much as possible

Checklists minimize errors of omission, provide better outcomes, and help most when stakes are high. You may feel like a novice when using a checklist, but experienced experts, including surgeons and pilots, use checklists too. Human memory, especially under stress, is too fallible to not use checklists.

Checklists are everywhere. For instance, enterprise software, like a CRM or a help ticket system, is just an interactive checklist: it tells you what to do and type.

5 How to Apologize Sincerely

Burning bridges refers to the act of damaging a relationship to the extent that one is no longer friendly to another. Here are examples of how people have burned bridges:

- Walked off a job
- Called the boss a jerk
- Shirked responsibility to provide an adequate transition to a successor because "all transitions are terrible"
- Poached talent from a friend

Have you done any of these things? If yes, then you burned a bridge. If you burned a bridge, it's okay. It happens more often than we'd like to admit. It's only possible to not burn bridges if you don't make relationships. That's not us; we are not that isolated.

So, you may have burned a bridge because you were:

- Young and immature
- Angry and pissed
- Lazy and entitled
- Clueless and unaware

If you burned a bridge, it's how you handle yourself afterward that counts. Apologize. No matter the circumstance, nothing can explain or excuse poor behavior.

Most of us hate apologizing because we want to preserve our belief that we're worthy and talented. In short, we're perfectionists.

Fight that urge. Instead, give a genuine apology. No sham apologies like "Thank you for the opportunity" or "I learned so much from you." These statements are not apologies; they are compliments and words of appreciation. A real apology sounds like:

- *I messed up.*
- *I acted unprofessionally.*
- *I did not meet your expectations, and it is my fault.*

Heartfelt words are an important first step. But that's not enough. A three to eleven-word apology, even a heartfelt one, feels insufficient for a monumental sin.

So, after uttering an apology, not only show penitence but also offer to make it right. Make the offer sincere and relevant. For instance, offering to write a transition document won't help if you walked off the job six months ago.

Apologies are hard, especially if it doesn't come naturally. But you'll be thankful that you tried. You'll need your boss' help for the next job opportunity: either as a reference or even a simple employment verification. And you'll sleep better at night, knowing that you took responsibility and did everything possible to right your wrong.

6 How to Play or Survive Politics

The word politics feels slimy, shady, and underhanded. However, politics will likely occur in a PM's career. PMs depend on engineers, designers, and other cross-functional team members to deliver results. Politics is about influencing others to get desired results.

PMs will encounter power as well. PMs get things done even when there is opposition. And power is about getting things done without unanimity.

Most people don't know what it means to play politics or how to do it. Others might be embarrassed that politics are a part of their arsenal, or they don't want you to learn their secrets.

I'll leave it to you to decide whether you'll use politics to get what you want. Either way, you need to at least be aware of it so that when these tactics are being used against you, you know what to do.

How One Establishes Power

To establish power, three parts need to occur:

1. Destabilize and overthrow the status quo
2. Establish the new regime
3. Sustain the new regime

Destabilizing the Status Quo

Tactic: Disparage others.

This common political tactic is one of the most effective and easiest to implement. Disparaging works because it is human nature to believe unsubstantiated criticism and negativity; we fear danger and the unknown.

Counter: Build an unassailable reputation well in advance, so that when the time comes, *others* will defend you.

Tactic: Undermine existing power bases.

Spawn your own power center by creating new organizations, committees, or task forces. After being forced out of the Lisa team in 1981, Jobs discovered the pre-existing Macintosh team. He seized control from Jef Raskin and established the Mac team as his new power center. Jobs then made the Mac division a new place to be. He fed that division with resources, his attention, and an exclusive, cult-like culture.

Like Jobs, John Sculley also undermined existing power bases by reorganizing the company. In 1984, he folded the Mac team back into Apple's groups, the year before Jobs was ousted from Apple.

Counter: Exile those you want to undermine.

Tactic: Incite disorder.

Organizational disorder leads to fear. And fearful constituents will clamor for a *new* leader to re-establish order.

There are many ways to incite disorder including spreading false information, overextending employees, and vacillating rules and responsibilities.

Counter: Proactively share clear and consistent information along with clear and reasonable roles.

Establish the New Regime

Tactic: Control resources.

Leaders cannot hold onto their position in a regime if they do not provide value. Controlling resources is the most common tactic. It could be access to:

- Budget
- Headcount
- Information
- Key influencers

Tactic: Build a small ruling coalition.

Borrowing other people's influence, via coalition, is a common tactic. At Facebook, Sheryl Sandberg's alliance with Mark Zuckerberg conveyed power and authority that she could not otherwise have.

When building a coalition, keep it small. Sounds counterintuitive, no? Shouldn't bigger be better?

Here's why you want a small ruling coalition: it minimizes the number of people the leader needs to stay in power. For instance, many have wondered why Theranos' disgraced CEO, Elizabeth Holmes, stayed in power for so long, despite having whistleblowers at almost every turn. It's because her small ruling coalition – consisting of herself, Sunny Balwani, and George Schultz – silenced them. In return, Holmes rewarded them for their loyalty.

Tactic: Keep your selectorate large.

For most companies, the board of directors serves as a check and balance on poor performing CEOs. Holmes' board of directors was notoriously weak because she kept her selectorate large.

She fielded her Board of Directors from the political and military world, led by former Secretary of State George Schultz. Holmes punished misbehaving board members by replacing them. The seemingly endless pool of retired, hands-off board candidates kept Holmes in power. Remaining board members learned their lesson; be loyal or receive punishment.

Maintain the New Regime

Tactic: Give favors.

Reward key members of your coalition by giving favors. For example, Lawrence Wasinger offered to chauffeur his big boss to work. The big boss, in return, rewarded him with a private 1:1 meeting during the commute. Lawrence gleaned privileged information and lobbied for his personal interests.

Counter: Appeal to rules, fairness, and due process. Institute organizational checks and balances to minimize favors.

Tactic: Take credit for another's work.

Others can demonstrate their value by taking credit for your work.

Counter: Make clear, proactively, what you've created. Your opponents will think twice about claiming credit for work you've publicized.

Tactic: Blackmail.

Blackmail is about gaining a favorable benefit in exchange for not revealing compromising or damaging information.

Counter: Reduce the leverage others have on you. Minimize the amount of damaging personal information that can be revealed.

Tactic: Intimidation and other psychological manipulation.

Psychological manipulation is about getting what you want by exploiting others' psychological weaknesses. This includes:

- Shaming
- Intimidating
- Avoiding or isolating
- Seducing through flattery

Counter: Label the tactic when you're being manipulated. For example, "I feel like you've been avoiding me the last three weeks. Is it because I criticized your product roadmap?" Also, strengthen your psychological core to minimize your psychological needs including the need for attention, achievement, or belonging.

7 Affirm Yourself

In the 1990s, Saturday Night Live had a sketch with a fictional character, Stuart Smalley. The sketch mocked the self-help phenomenon by having Stuart repeat his favorite mantra: "I'm good enough, I'm smart enough, and doggone it, people like me." Sounds corny, right?

Interestingly, the self-affirmation technique is grounded in science: Psychologist Martin Seligman coined the term "learned helplessness." He found that those who experienced a negative situation, were less likely to take control of future negative situations, even if they had the power to do something positive about it. In other words, those who suffered from a negative experience learned to be helpless.

If you've moved up the career ladder, you'll be presented with increasingly difficult situations. And you'll encounter failure. However, you must protect your psyche. You'll have to fight the natural tendency to be depressed and helpless.

The antidote to depression and learned helplessness can start with a daily affirmation. Say what you need to say to lift your mood and to empower yourself.

You may even exploit our understanding of the fundamental-attribution error. That is, flip it and knowingly blame the situation, but not yourself.

CHAPTER 7

Skill 5: Exceptional Team Builder

As a senior executive, one of the most important things you need to do is build strong, effective teams quickly. In this chapter, I've organized my team building tips under five key sections: hiring, onboarding, managing, promoting, and firing.

Hiring

1 The One Interview Question You Need to Ask

When interviewing candidates, there's one question you must ask: *Tell me a time when you handled criticism.*

From there, you need to look for three things:

1. Can they *receive* criticism?
2. Do they *act* after receiving criticism?
3. Do they *accept others' suggestions*?

Why is the criticism question important?

A fast-changing business environment needs people who can grow and adapt. According to Carol Dweck, those best suited to grow can take failure or negative feedback and:

- Face it
- Deal with it
- Learn from it

Dweck labels these special folks as having a "growth mindset."

Those with a growth mindset are different from those who grew up thinking they were smart and born "special." The special folks subsequently elude situations when they appear less special and smart. In other words, they hate and avoid failure. Furthermore, they:

- *Disagree with negative feedback*, sometimes silently
- *Neglect to act on negative feedback*

For these folks, negative feedback conflicts with their inner belief that they are special, talented, and capable.

What to look for in a good response?

When evaluating an answer to the criticism question, here's a checklist of things to look out for:

1. **Did they share an instance where they received *genuine criticism*?** Or did they share an insincere example?
2. **How did they react to the feedback?** Defensively? Did they acknowledge it as legitimate? Did they blame others or the situation? Or did they really understand their responsibility?
3. **What did they do about the feedback?** Did they change their behavior or sweep the matter under the rug? Put together a detailed, sincere, and thoughtful change plan? Did they adopt

others' suggestions? Or did they rebelliously reject those suggestions primarily because they wanted to come up with their *own* solution?

If you're doing it correctly, only 10 percent of individuals will answer the criticism question well.

The other 90 percent, who failed the question, will fall into two camps. One camp will resist the negative feedback. Another camp will not resist, but you'll find that they don't learn from or act on feedback. That's not good either.

Examples of Good Responses

Candidate Scenario	Growth-Mindset Response	Fixed-Mindset Response
Boss criticized my latest assignment	I immediately fixed the errors the way my boss wanted it because her feedback made sense. Separately, I learned more about the subject area on my own time, signing up for online courses and seeking out mentors. I know significantly more about the	I'm not sure if I messed up or not. Heck, my boss doesn't really know the situation. And even if I did mess up, things don't always go the way we want.

	topic now than I did two weeks ago when I first heard her criticism.	
Boss wanted me to take on a very technical project as a "growth opportunity"	I told her I'm up for the challenge, and I asked her, "How would you get up to speed if you were in my shoes?"	It's safer to say no. I don't want to fail.
I had a tense 1:1 with my direct report.	I told Rahul that if the last 1:1 felt awkward, it was probably my fault. I asked him if we could have a do-over because I feel he had some fair criticisms about the lack of role clarity on our team.	I should pretend it went well. After all, everyone fakes it until they make it.

Inspired by Julie Zhuo's *The Making of a Manager*

2 Work Simulations or Structured Interviews Work Best

Job interviews can be misleading. Candidates can train to say the right things.

Given that, what should we do when hiring new team members? Researchers Michael A. McDaniel and his collaborators – in their paper *The Validity of Employment Interviews* – give us valuable clues.

McDaniel indicates that the most effective method of identifying candidates is through a *work simulation* (which they call "situational interviews") followed by *structured interviews.* In a structured interview, questions are specified in advance and responses are scored according to a formal scoring guide.

Most interviews are what McDaniel calls "unstructured." That is, interviewers get to ask whatever they want and arbitrarily decide whether an answer is good or bad.

I will not specify what a work simulation or structured interview will look like for your organization. Every company's talent needs will differ.

So just remember this: when interviewing others, resist the temptation to improvise. Hiring someone just because they have the same hobbies or went to Ivy League schools isn't a recipe for success.

3 Always Check References

I am a big fan of reference checks because I'm wary of interviews.

I also believe that a person's past behavior is an indicator of future behavior. Old habits die hard. I've observed – over and over – that an individual doesn't change or adapt as quickly as he thinks.

When hiring internal candidates, external reference checks may be less useful. Those hiring managers can access past performance reviews or informally chat with former bosses instead. However, when hiring external candidates, reference checks are a precious opportunity to chat with someone who's seen your candidate's work first-hand.

Here are the four questions I ask when calling references:

1. What's your working relationship with the candidate?

2. Tell me about the candidate's strengths.

3. Tell me about the candidate's weaknesses.

4. Is there anything else you'd like to add?

What's your working relationship with the candidate?

The relationship question establishes context. Is this a friend? Or boss?

I strongly prefer former bosses as references. When candidates don't list former bosses it's a red flag. I wonder if they are still on good terms. Avoid those who aren't.

Some candidates do list former bosses, but the ex-boss doesn't reply. That's a red flag too. While it can happen, being busy is not a credible excuse. Bosses rush to sing praises of their top (or favorite) performers. Why? They're either indebted or think fondly of them. Bosses, who are grateful to ex-employees, do not disregard them during their time of need.

I also want to know whether the reference had first-hand exposure to the candidate's work. It's the work, not reputation or charisma, that's pertinent.

Tell me about the candidate's strengths.

The strengths question helps me understand what the candidate will bring to the job.

Top performers have a consistent and unmistakable strength. For example:

Individual	Consistent & Unmistakable Strength
Steph Curry	Quick 3-point shooter
Magic Johnson	Amazing passer
Shaquille O'Neal	Dominant post player

In my experience, top performers rarely, if ever, have inconsistent references. These top performers are so good that it's clear what strength the candidate will bring every single day.

Beware of references who provide lukewarm, meaningless compliments such as:

- *He's nice.*
- *He has a smile that brightens the room.*
- *He's smart. Look at his resume, he went to Harvard Business School.*

This behavior is indicative of a reference who is:

- **Avoiding the question**. They have nothing positive to say.
- **Lacking first-hand experience with the candidate**. They mention only the superficial.

One last note: ask the reference to share a story where the candidate demonstrated a strength. The story serves as evidence; it also indicates the rating of that strength.

Tell me about the candidate's weaknesses.

Many references hate this question. Nobody wants to accidentally torpedo a candidate's chances. Don't be surprised if they say: *Nothing* or *I don't know* or *Can't think of any.*

About 15 to 20 percent of the time, the reference will give a clue that merits more investigation like:

- *She's a fast worker, but **I wish she took more initiative or help others**.*
- *He's smart, but **he doesn't manage stress well**.*

- *He's well-liked, but **he wears his emotions on his sleeve**.*
- *She's a team player, but **she's not strategic**.*

Each "but" is an emotional code phrase that cloaks how a reference truly feels about the person.

Don't expect the reference to reveal the whole story. References want to keep things professional; few want to harm another, even if that person's work is poor.

So, ask more clarifying questions. Conduct more reference calls. Or invite the candidate to additional rounds of interviews.

The extra scrutiny is worth it. Uncover the secrets now, not later.

An Alternative Way of Checking References

My Kellogg professor had a quirky way of checking references. He suggested that we leave voicemails to a backchannel ex-manager to the effect of "My name is Lewis. We're considering ___ for the ___ role. We think they'd be a great hire. If you think we're making the right decision, call me back."

It's not an approach that I personally use. However, it does underscore a point I wholeheartedly agree with: Managers will take time out of their busy schedule to wholeheartedly endorse A+ (and even A) players. If you're having a hard time getting an ex-manager to return your calls, it's a signal that something is amiss.

4 Great Individuals Do Exist

Have you met someone of accomplishment and renown, only to conclude that the person was seemingly ordinary?

Here's the news flash: As ordinary as your co-workers may seem, I'm here to tell you that extraordinary individuals *are* in our midst.

(Space intentionally left blank)

Take for example this recent employee ranking exercise by my team:

Relative Performance of Employees

Compared to Baseline Employee A

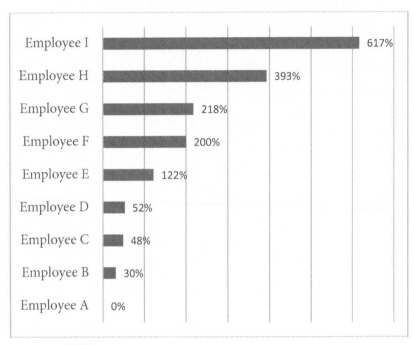

Source: Lewis C. Lin

Here's where it's different: Most stack ranks evaluate the *relative position* of each individual but doesn't tell us *how much better* one person is relative to another. This exercise does.

This group was randomly sampled from a large pool. Here's the interesting thing: the best employee outperforms the baseline employee by an astounding 617 percent! Talent is not homogeneous; differences between one employee and another is not minuscule. And keep in mind that this is a small team of nine. We can expect top performers to have a more outsized impact with a larger sample like 10,000.

If top performers are significantly better than average performers, why do the top performers feel so ordinary? The problem is that we often do not have first-hand observations into someone's work. Only a few close collaborators have that privilege. We typically form our opinions based on what others say or our first-hand experiences, with that individual, at social events.

Making the situation worse, most companies do not have objective stats for individual performance. What's the corporate equivalent to a basketball player's stat line of points, assists, rebounds, and blocks per game?

Here's the main takeaway: Don't settle for performance assessment without numbers. Define appropriate metrics, compare individual performance, and reward your best performers accordingly. Don't make the mistake of hiring, firing, or promoting the wrong person.

Onboarding

5 Your New Team Members Will Struggle & Here's Why

Consider this example. A new employee joins a team. He delivers early wins or has a winsome personality. Either way, he quickly becomes a team favorite. However, the initial honeymoon period doesn't last: the new employee is no longer the all-star that first joined the team. He becomes withdrawn or, in some cases, belligerent. The luster is gone. You can't help but imagine: What happened? Did we make a hiring mistake?

This post-honeymoon discomfort might sound familiar: it's the first sign of adversity between the new employee and his manager.

Adapting to a new team is not easy. 30 percent of new employees quit within the first 90 days[6]. In fact, some companies capitalize on this insight; they offer new employees $5,000 to quit the company[7].

Is this normal? According to Kenneth Blanchard, it is. When new employees join teams, they undergo four stages starting from orientation, dissatisfaction, resolution, and production (ODRP)[8]:

---

[6] Source: Jobvite

[7] Amazon and its subsidiary, Zappos, offers $5,000 to any employee who wishes to leave the company in the first few weeks.

[8] Source: *The One Minute Manager Builds High Performing Teams* by Kenneth Blanchard, Donald Carew, and Eunice Parisi-Carew

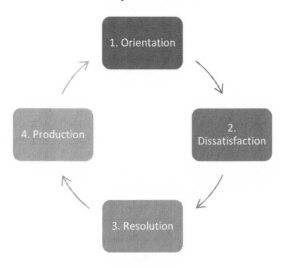

Blanchard's ODRP model tells us that we shouldn't expect new employees to be happy. And managers shouldn't expect their teams to be high performing on day 1.

Phase 1 - Orientation

New team members start the orientation phase with anticipation. It's their dream job! Life-changing events await!

First, it's a game of who's who. Who can I trust? Who's influential and powerful? And who's a fraud?

A few days into the job, anxiety kicks in. Where do you fit? What should you do? Can you live up to your bosses' great expectations?

Next, you wonder: what must you do? And what corners can you cut?

Finally, you accept that the new situation is just unfamiliar. You were a superhero on your old team. On this new team, you're powerless to make the same kind of impact. Never mind saving the world. It's easiest and safest to just suppress any shred of independent thinking. Just align with the corporate hierarchy and follow orders.

Top Needs during Phase 1

- **Establishing norms**. In other words, what are the common behaviors? Can I flout the in by 8:30 am and out at 5:30 pm workday?
- **Clarifying values**. In other words, what are the common beliefs? For example, does the company tolerate making mistakes so that we can move quickly? Or would the company rather we move deliberately to prevent rework?
- **Specifying goals**. In other words, what business objectives are we trying to achieve? A revenue goal? Customer acquisition goal? Engagement goal?

Phase 2 - Dissatisfaction

Dissatisfaction sets in. This is not the dream job you had hoped. It's just another corporate job with a top-down, authoritative hierarchy.

You grouse to close friends and family: you can do more and make a bigger impact if you simply had the freedom to do so. The company's approval processes would insult a five-year-old.

And the goals and processes: they're all wrong! No wonder this company is failing. If only the executives spent time outside of their bubble, then any off-the-street MBA could tell them how to save their company.

Or you may feel a little less indignant, but you're still dissatisfied and frustrated. You can't meet your bosses' expectations. You've tried everything, and nothing fixes the situation. You're confused and feeling incompetent. Depression crawls in.

Filled with dissatisfaction, you protest by confronting others or withdrawing silently. Publicly or privately, you question whether you belong. This so-called dream job: you don't know what it is anymore. You've stopped caring.

Top Needs during Phase 2

- *Mentoring* to work through the dissatisfaction
- *Providing* space to rationalize dissatisfaction on their own time

Special Notes

Bruce Tuckman found that 85 percent of new team members experience the dissatisfaction phase, and only 50 percent of those successfully overcome their dissatisfaction.

Phase 3 - Resolution

Resolution starts with introspection: new employees realize they've spent too much time blaming the boss or the company. Yes, this new team is littered with brick walls. But maybe brick walls aren't the problem. Every company has obstacles.

Maybe the problem is you. You're missing the skills to jump, go around, or break through the brick wall. In other words, your frustration is an opportunity to learn new skills and handle adversity in the future.

Your boss may not be the best, but you can see how she could be worse. You realize you can tolerate her, at least until the next reorganization, which is probably just a couple months away. In the meantime, there are plenty of new experiences and skills to acquire and learn.

You're also more forgiving toward the company. Who doesn't want their company to be stronger, faster, and leaner? But you recognize change is tougher than it seems. And after hearing more about their corporate history, you realize the company has made significant strides recently.

Your maturity pays off. Your newfound sense of individual accountability, coupled with a more tolerant and forgiving attitude, clears – or at least sets aside – your emotional baggage. Your projects no longer seem like a chore. Your protests subside. There's more harmony in your interpersonal relationships.

Personal wins begin again.

Your boss isn't the one-dimensional corporate figure you feared. She reveals more strengths, which engenders your respect. You've even re-established trust with her; you feel more open with her and the team. It feels less like me vs. them, and more like us.

The trust, support, and respect – that you give and receive – makes a difference. You open up. You're more comfortable speaking up, proposing ideas, and sharing criticism. You tell yourself: this new team is starting to feel like family.

Top Needs during Phase 3

Giving space for the team to operate

Phase 4 - Production

The new team is humming beautifully. The work may be hard, but you realize you've never been part of a team that's performed so capably.

Everyone plays a clear role. It's the workplace version of knowing what they're going to say and how they're going to say it. Best friends forever!

You have complete trust from your boss. Sometimes she takes the lead; other times, you take the lead. When obstacles come in your way, you don't doubt your team's ability to overcome it.

And the wins come so effortlessly now. When obstacles come, you're buoyed by your most recent achievement.

"Pinch me now," you say. You're living the dream. And all the early frustrations make it so much sweeter. There's nothing this team can't do.

Top Needs during Phase 4

Letting your team be amazing

6 Overcoming Adversity with New Team Members

There are a couple of implications from the ODRP model.

Set expectations at the very beginning

Good leaders establish, communicate, and enforce high standards. Bad leaders tolerate low standards. I've found it helpful to share the ODRP phases to help teams understand dissatisfaction is normal. It also helps managers facilitate conversations around job satisfaction.

Wait for the first sign of adversity

Duped by a new person's charisma or early wins, some managers make the mistake of promoting too early. Wait instead for the first moment of adversity. How does he respond? Here are some behaviors to look for:

Positive Behaviors	Negative Behaviors
Bounces back from adversity	Add to or hide from adversity
Takes personal accountability	Blames others or the situation
Stops detrimental behavior	Continues detrimental behavior
Builds knowledge and skills	Avoids new knowledge or skills
Recommits themselves to the role	Plans exit from the company

You'll notice that I'm exalting individuals who:

- Are **open to criticism** and **treats the criticism as valid**
- Not only **bounce back from failure** but also **find positives from negative events**
- **Do not quit** when others might
- Create and commit themselves to a **self-improvement plan**

These kinds of individuals are very rare. If they triumph over their adversity go ahead and promote them. You won't regret it because you'll want to keep them for a very long time. We'll call them growth-minded individuals.

Hire those who triumph over adversity

Over the years, I've seen exceptional individuals – in one domain – switch roles and become exceptional in another domain.

Daniel Kahneman made a similar observation during his time with the Israel Defense Forces (IDF). The IDF tasked him to create a personality test to determine ideal roles for incoming military members.

His conclusion: it doesn't matter. High potential individuals would be outstanding in any role – as a fighter pilot, sharpshooter, or cyber intelligence expert.

Many companies implicitly follow Kahneman's rule: they prefer hiring military veterans, Olympic gold medalists, or other individuals with notable distinction. Hiring managers understand an Olympic archer's bow-and-arrow skills would not be useful as a product manager. Instead, they prefer these individuals because they've learned how to face adversity, bounced back, dug in, and triumphed.

You may have heard the saying, "Hire for attitude. Train for skill." Hiring for attitude doesn't mean hire a social butterfly who can enchant you with a story. What it really means is to hire one with a growth mindset.

You can train someone to write user stories or extract data from a database. The team will reap the benefit within days. But for those who don't have a growth attitude, cultivating that can take a decade or longer. No hiring manager can wait that long.

So, hire for those with a growth attitude. And train everything else.

Five Things to Look for When Hiring for Growth-Mindset

Characteristic	Questions to Ask
Open to criticism	Do they get defensive?
Resiliency	Do they wallow in self-pity? Or are they ready to resume life as normal?
Accepts adversity	Do they make the most of their situation? Or do they complain that the grass is greener on the other side?

Adapts quickly	Do they default to tactics and behaviors they've used in the past? Or are they willing to try new tactics, risking failure and embarrassment?
Learns new skills	What do they do with feedback? Do they learn new skills? Or do they simply just try harder? Most importantly, do they accept others' suggestions?
Masters new skills	Have they mastered the new skills they've learned?

7 Set High Expectations for Your Team

John Wooden's record of excellence is remarkable, especially since his players change from year to year.

Wooden was known for having high expectations. He asked his star players to shave their beards and keep their hair trimmed. And he required players to wear socks a certain way.

During the "anything goes" 1960s, it was unusual for Wooden to enforce high expectations. But he knew his expectations positively affected team performance. For instance, putting socks on incorrectly led to blisters. Blisters meant injuries. And players could not perform if they were injured.

Like Wooden, the best PM leaders set high expectations, even on trivial matters, because it impacts performance and leaders are responsible for results. High expectations also *communicate* what it means to perform well and commit us to an endeavor.

Peter Drucker had a fascinating insight: he believed that "people grow according to the demands they make on themselves." If you expect little, people will do little. If you expect a lot, people will achieve a lot.

The human spirit often rises to the occasion.

Managers and team members alike resist setting high expectations, despite the benefits. Here's why:

- **Fear**. All of us fear failure. Instinctually, we crave social acceptance. Why set high goals, where we increase our chances of disappointing others? Practically, we fear the consequences of not meeting goals: demotions and getting fired.
- **Ignorance and lack of imagination**. If we don't know an alternate way to put on our socks, we assume that it's not possible.
- **Indifference and negligence**. We don't bother to investigate an alternate way to put on socks because we assume that it doesn't matter.

One last reminder, setting high expectations can be frightful. So be supportive and respectful.

8 Don't Rush to Do Team-Building Exercises

Inexperienced team builders rush to do team-building activities. Experienced team-builders delay.

Why? While team building strengthens relationships, experienced leaders may not want to do so, especially when they expect existing team members to leave soon.

I'm not saying that you should avoid team meetings completely; however, be mindful of the consequences when introducing team-building activities with a short-lived team.

Managing

9 Praise Groups in Public, but Individuals in Private

Conventional wisdom says employees crave (public) recognition for their work.

So, your typical manager heeds the advice and praises *individuals* in public. Shortly after, team morale drops unexpectedly. What happened?

Those who were recognized feel good. But those who weren't can't help feeling:

- Jealous
- Underappreciated
- Being on the wrong side of favoritism

The managers are at a loss. They thought they should be commended for recognizing others now find a disheartened team.

What should managers do instead? Praise is good. Most managers don't do it enough. But if you're going to praise in public, praise the group. If you plan to praise an individual, do it in private.

10 Strive for Clear, Actionable, and Accurate Feedback

Robert Duvall is a legendary movie actor. During an interview with Oprah, he remarked how far modern directors have come when it comes to giving feedback: Duvall recalled one director who once told him, "When I say 'Action!' – tense up!"

While it is actionable, the director's feedback wasn't clear. Where should Duvall tense up? And how? And to what degree? And most importantly, why did Duvall need to tense up?

Push for Clarity

Like Duvall's director, most managers give inadequate feedback. So, challenge yourself as a manager:

- Accurate feedback is rare.
- Clear feedback is rarer.
- Actionable feedback is the rarest.

Your people deserve all three. Practice diagnosing issues, describing issues, and prescribing fixes.

Don't Be Too Nice

Many managers, even experienced ones, make the mistake of not providing feedback to underperformers. The most common refrain: Why hurt their feelings when I should encourage the underperformer?

Here's the tip: underperformers will *always* find out about their poor performance. It'll happen when you:

- Fire them
- Decline their promotion
- Give them a poor performance review

And their response will invariably be: "Why didn't you tell me sooner?"

The underperformers are right. You have a responsibility to tell them that they are underperforming. It's about being clear and transparent in communications. It's about not leading them on under a false pretense. And it's also about hope: with that improved feedback, they might improve their performance.

11 Delegate, Delegate, Delegate

It's a blessing when you can delegate to a team. Delegating increases your team's throughput. It reduces burnout by balancing tasks across a larger number of people. Lastly, delegating allows you to spend more time thinking[9] and less time doing.

The most common delegation mistake is not delegating enough. The usual refrain: "Why delegate a task when it's faster to do it myself? The output will be of higher quality too." We also refrain from delegating because we worry about losing control and missing opportunities to showcase our value.

There's also a significant setup cost when delegating to others. However, by not taking the time to teach others, you forgo an opportunity to free your time to focus on something more important.

Focus on the long-term benefits and ignore the short-term productivity decrease. Let's say it takes you an hour to do a task. Assume the new person will take two hours to do it:

- They'll attempt the task in the first hour.
- You'll teach, fix, or redo the task in the second hour.

---

[9] I am not suggesting this so that leaders can avoid doing work. Thinking, planning, and strategizing – if you haven't realized already – is difficult. It is far easier to do than to determine what to do and why we should do it. Teams expect their leaders to do the thinking and provide guidance.

As a leader, you should rarely do the same task more than a few times. There are always new problems that demand your attention and problem-solving skills. Delegate aggressively so you have time to focus on the new.

12 Create Delegation Recipes

Researchers Robert E. Kelley and Dick Hayes analyzed novice, experienced, and expert tech employees. They found that novice employees generate ten different hypotheses to a problem and then exhaustively (and tediously) investigate each one. Experts, however, would generate 10 to 15 different hypotheses, but quickly weed those hypotheses down to one or two for investigation. In other words, experts saved a lot of time. Most importantly, the experts' accuracy was very high.

Kelley and Hayes' research went further: experts spent 20 percent of their total project hours in this investigation phase (which they called "discovery"), wasting a scant 2 percent of it. Experienced engineers and novices would spend 50 and 60 percent of total project hours in the investigation phase, wasting 30 and 43 percent of that time, respectively.

To help your team perform their best, minimize the amount of time team members investigate a new problem or project. In other words, avoid having them re-invent the wheel.

One of the best ways of doing so is by creating step-by-step recipes with visuals. These delegation recipes:

- Save your team from creating processes from scratch
- Minimize errors by serving as a checklist
- Conserve time because you can re-use the same recipe when training others

- Identify future process improvements easily

13 How to Delegate the Right Tasks

The second most common delegation mistake: managers delegate tasks they should keep and keep tasks they should delegate.

For instance, many managers are accustomed to having junior employees present to executives. They want to reward staff members with executive face time. And some managers feel guilty or uncomfortable presenting someone else's work.

This approach can be appropriate for a low-risk presentation presided by a caring, supportive executive. However, executive presentations are rarely low-risk situations. Executives are impatient. They will erupt if you waste their time with a shaky, half-baked presentation. Additionally, you and your boss's reputation is on the line. Neither one of you wants to be embarrassed by a junior employee on your team.

(Space intentionally left blank)

A Delegation Framework

To decide when to delegate, I've found Keith Rabois' framework help-ful[10]:

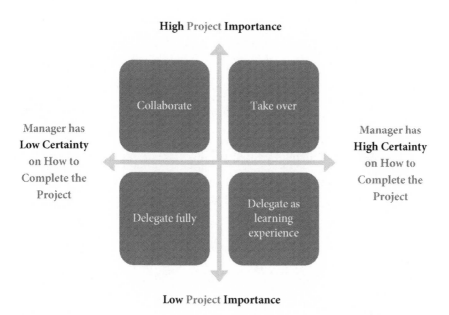

You may be shocked by Rabois' recommendation to "take over." It sounds authoritarian. However, it reveals the most important insight of Rabois' model: you can delegate tasks, but you can never delegate accountability. Regardless of who does the work, you are always responsible. Hence, when the stakes are high, you must step in and do everything in your power to deliver the desired results and behaviors.

---

[10] Rabois reminds us that, when evaluating new talent, we shouldn't immediately shun leaders who are perceived as micromanagers or perceived as hands-off. As long as they're applying the correct leadership style in a given situation, their micromanagement or hands-off style may be okay.

Assign Existing Projects to New Members

When assigning projects to new team members, I strongly prefer giving them existing, rather than new, projects. Here's why:

1. **Clear scope and instructions**. New team members will appreciate working on a well-defined project.
2. **Available training.** There will be at least two team members – the existing project owner and the boss – who can provide training and guidance. They can also monitor their work and help when needed.
3. **Save greenfield projects for existing team members**. I'd much rather have an existing, not new, team member work on a greenfield project. Those projects are uncertain. An existing team member with a demonstrated skillset, established relationships, and strong familiarity with the corporate culture will be more likely to succeed.

14 See One, Do One, Teach One

"See one, do one, teach one" is an oft-heard mantra at medical schools. It is how many med students learn how to become a doctor.

Here's how it works: a med student "sees one" by shadowing a physician who is delivering a baby. Then the med student "does one" by delivering a baby on his own. Finally, a med student "teaches one" by teaching another student how to deliver a baby.

It may be shocking that this is how high-paying doctors get trained. Set aside those fears for now. "See one, do one, teach one" reminds us that this mantra is an effective way to get a novice up to speed. It harkens back to the apprenticeship model, something that's been proven over the centuries, which seems to be forgotten in today's sink-or-swim culture.

15 Meetings

Jeff Bezos, Robert McNamara, and Peter Drucker believe that a well-managed company should be boring. No drama. And no excess meetings.

To them, a meeting-happy culture implies a poorly managed organization. It could indicate apathy. Or wrong-headed acceptance of a meeting-heavy culture. Or perhaps inadequately defined processes, roles, and responsibilities.

So keep that in mind: Meetings should be the exception, not the rule. External meetings with clients and partners are okay. Otherwise, too many meetings could be a symptom of mal-organization.

16 Minimize Anchoring Bias during Performance Reviews

Most hiring managers start performance reviews by letting their direct reports go first: *How do you think you performed during the review period?*

By doing so, they've unwittingly put themselves in a hole! The employee establishes a perception anchor. The managers must now correct that perception, which is usually incorrect, especially with underperformers.

And because of anchoring bias, managers have difficulty adjusting from that anchor. In other words, when managers intended to mark someone as a low performer, inadvertently gets marked as an average performer, because the gap between high performance (employee's assessment) and low performance (manager's assessment) is too large!

So, don't fall into that trap. Don't expect employees to be aware and correct in their self-assessment. Go first. Set the record straight.

17 Shared Activities

My favorite type of networking is when one has an opportunity to demonstrate value.

However, networking, by spending time with another, is valuable too. Whether it's a weekly ritual to share food and drink or playing a weekly tennis game, it's an opportunity to:

- Gain familiarity
- Build shared history
- Exchange information

Promoting

18 Promote the Internal Candidate That's 60 Percent Ready

My Kellogg professor had a philosophy: The well-liked internal candidate who is 60 percent ready may be a better hire than the hotshot external candidate who is closer to 100 percent ready.

Why? On the one hand, team members may resent and undermine the external hotshot. On the other hand, members will support the well-liked internal candidate.

It's another reminder that getting things done requires teams. Teamwork is about relationships. No hotshot can get things done on his or her own.

One last thing, having a well-liked internal candidate is insufficient. You must be confident that this person can learn and acquire the missing skills too.

Firing

19 Don't Give Up Too Early, but Don't Wait Too Long Either

Managers can make the mistake of holding onto poor-performing team members for too long. They can also make the mistake of giving up on them too easily. Do your best to make the pieces fit. Do your best to help team members get better. But after you've given it your best shot, sometimes the best course for you and the rest of the team is to simply let the new person go.

The decision to fire is debilitating. No one wants to fire another.

Ultimately, every manager is accountable for results. The most helpful question I ask when making the firing decision is this: "If the role were open, would I hire the current person – with the additional information I have now – or would I take a chance on someone else?" If the answer is the latter, then it's time to move on.

Skill 6: Moonshot Vision

A moonshot vision is an ambitious, groundbreaking product vision. It feels as audacious as John F. Kennedy's 1961 proclamation to land the first humans on the moon.

Here are more examples of outstanding moonshots:

- SpaceX (2002): enable human life on Mars
- Google (1998): organize the world's information
- Microsoft (1980): a computer on every desk and every home

Why are moonshot visions important?

Having a moonshot vision is a good strategy.

Starting with marketing strategy, marketers overwhelm consumers with promotional messages. A customer typically remembers one thing about a company, so make it unique and memorable. If several companies have a mission to go to space, being the only space company *flying to Mars* stands out.

Onto competitive strategy, a moonshot vision cleverly opens a distant battlefront, out of an incumbent's reach. An incumbent can't easily pursue a competitor's moonshot vision because it involves unfamiliar capabilities, customers, or regulations. The incumbents will traverse the same steep learning curve as the new entrant.

However, incumbents will learn more slowly. Why? They are distracted. They're busy maintaining their current product portfolio or servicing existing customers. Free from these burdens, new entrants outrun the incumbents, despite the incumbents' illusory strengths.

What happens to companies without clear, compelling moonshot visions?

Two noted academics, Jim Collins and Tom Peters attempted to identify enduring, high performing companies. You'd be surprised that their list of 50 enduring companies includes:

- *Defunct companies* like Circuit City and Digital Equipment
- *Middling companies* like IBM and Hewlett-Packard

Even the most admirable brand names on their lists – American Express and Walmart – are not considered to be the most groundbreaking companies in finance or retail.

So what did Collins and Peters miss in their analysis?

I'd argue the companies on their lists were no longer captained by a CEO with a moonshot vision. You'll find that almost all the companies, from Circuit City to Walmart, had an audacious moonshot vision during their early days. However, as they passed the early and middle part of the innovation S-curve, their incremental improvements provided diminishing returns. Other competitors then caught up and provided similar products. That triggered product commoditization, leading to lower prices and stagnant growth.

One last confirmation: we see that IBM and HP's mission statements are far from the aspirational moonshot visions I shared from Google, Microsoft, and Tesla earlier:

- IBM: To lead in the creation, development, and manufacture of the industry's most advanced information technologies, including computer systems, software, networking systems, storage devices and microelectronics.
- HP: We earn customer respect and loyalty by consistently providing the highest quality and value.

Delight the Customer

Good product development begins by clarifying the goal. Moonshot companies can choose a practical goal like ROI. But that's not the right choice.

The best CEOs know that there's only one choice, and it's delighting the customer.

Consider any remarkable company – such as Apple, Amazon, Google, Tesla – and you'll find that delighting the customer was at its core, at least in its early days.

A remarkable company loses its way when it neglects the customer and prioritizes goals that are not as customer-focused such as:

- Curtailing piracy
- Minimizing waste
- Growing share of wallet
- Minimizing cannibalism

- Increasing sales of complementary goods

Customers will tolerate neglect for only so long. Eventually, they'll give up and move onto the next option, especially if it's superior.

2 Figure Out What Customers Want Before They Do

Some people say, "Give the customers what they want." But that's not my approach. Our job is to figure out what they're going to want before they do. I think Henry Ford once said, "If I'd asked customers what they wanted, they would have told me, 'A faster horse!'"

People don't know what they want until you show it to them. That's why I never rely on market research. Our task is to read things that are not yet on the page.

– Steve Jobs

Steve Jobs figured out what customers want, without asking, because he empathized with his customers. To empathize, one must understand what people say and how people act, think, and feel.

To gain empathy, Jobs pursued experiences unfamiliar to him but were familiar to others. For example, Jobs:

- Traveled to India & Japan
- Enrolled in calligraphy classes
- Obsessed over motherboard design

These unique experiences allowed Jobs to see things from someone else's perspective.

We can deduce why Jobs wasn't a fan of market research or talking to customers. It's hard for customers, let alone anyone, to articulate the perfect solution. It is easy, however, for customers to point out and request features that competitors have but yours don't.

(We shouldn't be surprised when competitors copy one another. Their customers are asking them to do so!)

Talking to customers can also be expensive and time-consuming to coordinate.

So, conjure a product vision that's unique, innovative, and bold. Don't shy away because you're afraid of failing or being wrong. Don't expect your customers or your market research team to hand it to you. They can't, even if they wanted to.

3 Inspiration Comes First

Moonshot visions do not spontaneously form. Instead, inspiration sparks vision. Your job, as guardian of the moonshot vision, is to collect good ideas. The more you have, the more you can be inspired by.

You can collect ideas from anywhere: traveling to a new city, visiting a museum, or reading extensively. Time Magazine's Best Inventions of the Year issue is one of my favorite sources for inspiration. Also, science fiction fans have long mined their favorite sci-fi books for inspiration. For instance:

Innovation	First Appeared...	...In this Sci-Fi Work
Credit Cards, popularized in the 1950s	1888	*Looking Backward* by Edward Bellamy
Atomic Power, popularized in the 1940s	1914	The World Set Free by H.G. Wells

Robots, used in manufacturing starting in the 1980s	1920	Rossum's Universal Robots, a play by Karel Čapek
Earbuds, popularized in the 1980s	1953	*Fahrenheit 451* by Ray Bradbury
Self-driving cars, aggressively developed in the 2000s	1953	Sally, a short story by Issac Asimov
Cell phones, popularized in the 1990s	1964	Communicators used by Star Trek officers

To collect inspiration effectively, push yourself to be curious anytime, anywhere. Inspiration can come from the unlikeliest of places. For example, you could be walking your dog, look up at a streetlamp, and get inspired on how to make it better.

4 Copy the Thinking, not the Product

It's not enough to see the inspiration, you must smell it, touch it, and even take it apart. In other words:

- What was the inventor's original goal?
- What were the constraints?
- What were the alternative ways of achieving the goal? Why didn't the inventor pursue one of the alternatives?

When copying your role models, think of yourself as Vincent Van Gogh, painting his renowned Sunflowers, inspired by Monet's Sunflowers, painted a couple of years before. Do not imitate stroke by stroke. The goal is not to pass off your work as a Monet. The goal, when copying, is to understand.

Like an art study, internalize deeply the problems and solutions when creating the final product. That is, how does light color, perspective, medium, and audience affect your art?

As you copy to learn, also ask yourself: What would Steve Jobs or Jeff Bezos do? That question may illuminate solutions that may not be apparent to you.

The reason we want to copy the thinking and not the product is because we must *learn how to approach the problem for our specific situation*. Your industry, resources and customers could be very different from Jobs and Bezos'.

For example, after World War 2, Ford and GM inspired a then struggling Toyota. However, Toyota could not copy Ford and GM's manufacturing processes. Compared to Ford and GM, Toyota's labor pool was significantly more expensive; Toyota's workers could not be fired either. Adapting what they learned, Toyota ended up building their own manufacturing philosophy, the legendary Toyota Production System.

You shouldn't feel guilty about using someone else's inspiration. Steve Jobs derived inspiration from a variety of sources including:

Iconic Jobs' Innovation	Original Inspiration
Mac GUI	Xerox PARC
Mac OS X	Carnegie Mellon's Mach Kernel
iPod's Click Wheel Browsing Interface	Creative's NOMAD II Jukebox
iTunes Software	Casady and Greene's SoundJam, purchased by Apple one year after the release

iPhone's "Pinch to Zoom" gesture	Samsung's Diamond Touch Touchscreen

Perhaps Jobs' knew that Monet's creation was just a starting point for Van Gogh. As he innovated, Jobs incorporated his own goals, constraints, and his unique blend of strengths. Jobs' resulting products ended up very different from the original.

One last thing, while inspiration is important, I do not want you to wait for a divine event. Xerox PARC is not waiting to open their pearly gates so you can steal the next big thing. Instead, to paraphrase Yohji Yamamoto, just get going. Copy copy copy. If you copy long enough, you will find yourself and your moonshot vision.

5 Innovation is a Volume Game

Even the great Steve Jobs could not consistently generate successful product visions.

Do you remember the Apple Lisa, Next, and the iMac G4 with the fragile sunflower-shaped monitor? Probably not. They were some of Steve Jobs' biggest failures.

So, if even the great Steve Jobs – who gave us the Mac, iPod, iPad, and the iPhone – could not consistently generate one successful product after another, then to have at least one amazing product, we must brainstorm and pursue lots of potential product ideas.

6 SCAMPER Toward a Solution

Refrain from implementing your first product vision. It's usually generic or uninspired. Or it may be too similar to an existing solution.

Instead, brainstorm at least 10 solutions. In my experience, truly creative ideas appear no sooner than the eighth idea.

There are many frameworks to help facilitate brainstorming. SCAMPER is easily my favorite framework. It's an acronym that stimulates our brainstorming:

	Can we create a new product by...	Example
Substitute	Substituting one element of an existing product	Instead of ridesharing for cars, how about ridesharing for boats?
Combine	Combining two products or concepts	What happens when you combine circus-like acrobatics with a Broadway musical experience?
Adapt	Re-adjust a product for another purpose	How can I adapt a tablet computer for a car?
Magnify or Minify	Put more / less emphasis or features	Instead of a seven-step checkout process, can we do it in one-step?
Put	Putting it to another use	Can facial recognition technology, currently used by law enforcement, help journalists pick out prominent US

		Congress members from a crowd?
Eliminate	Removing one or more elements of a current product	Other tablets have flat displays, touch screens, and handwriting recognition. What if we eliminated the handwriting feature?
Reverse	Reversing or rearranging the product or process	To test drive a car, instead of having car buyers going to the dealership, what if we have car dealers bring cars to buyers' homes?

And the simplest brainstorming framework: simply ask "Why not?" It's a favorite of many tech veterans:

- **Sergey Brin**: He once proposed the invention of a space elevator. When questioned "Why?" he replied with "Why not?"
- **Evan Spiegel**: He once asked his product teams, "Why not a phone without a ringer?" Aside from the fact that he truly felt it was possible, Evan's question pushed his teams to think differently.
- **Van Phillips**: Phillips was a biomedical engineer who wondered why foot prosthetics needed to look like a human foot. He wondered, why not a prosthetic that looks like a cheetah's foot? Phillips is the inventor of Flex-Foot, the prosthetics that were famously used by Olympian Oscar Pistorius.

7 Set a High Bar for Brainstorming

Common wisdom tells us to defer judgment when brainstorming, and I agree. When volume matters, judging and censoring ideas will reduce participation and volume. And after all, innovation is a volume game.

Nonetheless, researcher Adam Grant and others have found creativity is less effective in uncritical environments. Creativity is more productive where criticism is accepted or even requested.

So, find participants who accept and embrace criticism and then create a culture with high standards for innovation.

And one last tip from Adam Grant: participants are more open to criticism when there's an environment of trust.

8 Jump on Fast-Growing Trends & Ecosystems

Some of the best consumer marketers work at consumer-packaged-goods (CPG) companies like Nestlé and Procter & Gamble. Most CPG marketers have ingrained in their heads something that others do not: consumer insight is the key to innovation. Here are some examples:

Current trend...	Will increase demand for...
Increased life expectancy	Products aimed at 90-year olds
More home theaters with streaming media	Eating at home

In addition to consumer trends, moonshot owners need to pay attention to technology shifts. Each technology shift can uncover an opportunity goldmine. Consider these examples:

A new technology ecosystem based on...	Created a new opportunity to...	Which Led to...

Inexpensive, plentiful Internet bandwidth and storage	Store large video files	YouTube
Person-to-person online auctions	Pay sellers more effectively	PayPal
Smartphones with cameras	Take and share photos all the time	Instagram
Smartphones with GPS chips	Give all drivers an opportunity to be a cab driver	Uber

9 Design and Innovation is Not Sexy

I ask the creatives on my team, "What's the toughest part of your job?" Invariably the answer is brainstorming. I can't agree more.

Creativity is not a divine and rapturous event. Instead, it's painfully frustrating. Confusing. Ugly and messy.

But if you can enjoy the process (and refrain from fixating on your ugly and messy progress), you'll not only enjoy it more, but you'll persist longer than you would otherwise.

10 Watch Out for Resource Starvation

Every corporate historian can spin tales of woe.

For instance, there's the Xerox retiree who rues Xerox PARC's missed opportunity to dominate the PC industry, ultimately won by IBM, Microsoft, and Intel. Or the Microsoft lifer who bemoans Microsoft early Tablet PC and Windows Phone efforts, which were bested by Apple's iPad and iPhone.

There are many reasons why these companies could not capitalize on their first-mover advantage including market uncertainty, technology uncertainty, and steep learning curves.

However, for large corporations, like the Xerox and Microsoft examples above, the blame largely rests on under-resourcing massive growth opportunities they could not foresee.

Refrain from making similar mistakes. Give your growth opportunities the resources they need to succeed by:

1. **Eliminating distractions**. Unencumber your innovation teams from legacy obligations. This includes maintaining current products, servicing current customers, or bounding through bureaucratic processes.

2. **Assigning the best**. The skilled labor requirements for moonshots are uncertain. Thus, CEOs will want their best talent, with an array of skills, on moonshots. Unfortunately, the best employees are rarely given permission to pursue them. Their bosses are too possessive to let them go. As a result, executives assign the B team to moonshots.

3. **Providing cash and headcount**. There's no shortage of moonshot teams, trapped in the bowls of a large corporation, who do not have what they needed to compete successfully. They're stymied by a demanding CFO who rejected their budget request because the moonshot didn't exceed a hurdle rate or its revenue looked insignificant. Or they're being blocked by an influential executive because the team has been too busy to curry favor.

As you can infer, the cause of resource starvation is the parent company itself: distractions, difficult re-staffing top employees, and organizational bureaucracy choking off critical resource allocations.

Corporate spinoffs are my favorite tactic to overcome organizational barriers. Microsoft wisely spun off Expedia. And Expedia, in turn, spun off TripAdvisor too. Expedia and TripAdvisor, thanks to the spinoffs, got what they needed to succeed, without interference from a parent company.

11 No Renegade Efforts

Have a clear picture of how the new moonshot integrates with the core business. For example, YouTube videos supplement Google Search results. YouTube also adds new ad inventory for Google's advertisers.

Similarly, Prime's two-day shipping enhances Amazon's shopping experience. At the same time, it expands the competitive moat because the logistics and distribution infrastructure – fulfillment/sortation centers and delivery trucks/airplanes – makes it very costly for Amazon's competitors to copy.

Michael Porter argues that a good strategy is a set of mutually reinforcing activities that strengthen the business' core value proposition. Both YouTube and Amazon Prime meet Porter's definition.

12 What Happens When Efforts Aren't Integrated

During the 1980s, Steve Jobs' efforts to build a secret Mac division inside Apple exemplifies what happens when efforts aren't integrated. Jobs favored the Mac division: they had a special language, cultural code, perks, and privileges.

The Mac division fomented distrust with those outside of it. It bred resentment. Not only was it not clear how the Mac organization helped the rest of Apple, but it also accelerated Jobs' ouster in 1985, partly because Apple insiders could not tolerate his increasingly powerful Mac insurgency.

13 The Best Visionaries Get into Technical Details

In the mid-1980s, John Sculley, not Jobs, was Apple's leader. Back then, Apple was fighting for its life. IBM's PC ecosystem dwarfed Apple's. IBM PC clones were cheaper and had more options. Most importantly, PCs had a vast ecosystem of third-party applications.

By contrast, Apple didn't have an extensive app ecosystem. The most reliable Mac app developer was Apple's in-house software group named Claris, which focused on productivity software. Claris' apps felt inferior to the most important productivity apps at the time – Word-Perfect, Lotus 1-2-3, and dBase – all of which were unavailable for Mac.

Sculley wanted the Mac to run those business apps along with thousands of PC titles that weren't available for Mac. In other words, he wanted Macs to be IBM compatible.

However, his engineers scoffed. Impossible, they said. The Macs' Motorola chipset could not efficiently run applications optimized for PC clones; PCs were on a different chipset, the Intel 8086.

Sculley then asked whether an expansion card with an 8086 processor could be added to the Mac. His engineers scoffed again. It's not possible they said; the Mac didn't have any expansion slots. So Sculley gave up. Macs then trudged on without IBM compatibility and quickly became irrelevant.

Sadly, Sculley was right. Who wanted a computer that barely had any applications? And to vindicate Sculley, years after his departure, Macs gained cross-platform app compatibility when Apple released BootCamp and more so when the Internet gained popularity.

Elon Musk is the opposite of Sculley. Musk is an example of what moonshot visionaries should do: learn the technical details. At SpaceX, he read the fundamentals of propulsion, aerodynamics, thermodynamics, and gas turbines. In a spreadsheet, he dissected the components of building rockets.

From there, Musk proposed that SpaceX should build reusable rockets using commercial-grade, not space-grade technology. It would be cheaper and faster than buying rockets from governments. After explaining the technical details, his team accepted his proposal, largely because he showed his team *how* to build it, something Sculley did not do.

Engineers often criticize PMs for describing how a product should be built. I understand the argument; nobody likes to be told what to do. However, I'd argue that most engineers criticize PMs for suggesting how to build it because many PMs use a Sculley-like approach. That is, most PMs suggest a vision or feature without understanding the technical details. When asked – "How would you build it?" – PMs wilt.

14 Prioritize 40 Percent Innovations First

When prioritizing my innovation pipeline, I think to myself, "Will this improve my metrics by at least 40 percent?" I call these game-changing innovations "40 Percent Innovations."

It's a way to protect my development teams from working on less impactful innovations, ones that improve performance by a few percent here and a few percent there.

As moonshot visionaries, we need to be forever vigilant and wary of small evolutionary features. By default, most of our innovation pipeline is small features. Why? First, it's easier to propose small changes. They're the teeny requests that our customers ask for or jealously admire when reviewing our competitors' products. Second, 40 percent of innovations are scary. Why propose a big bet that most likely won't work?

Nonetheless, there are two more reasons why we need to look for 40 percent innovations:

1. To delight our customers (and deliver the growth our shareholders expect), we need to do something big.
2. Our product portfolio will invariably have losers, and to come out ahead, we need some big winners.

15 How to Handle Criticism

If you're trying to suggest a new product idea (or building a new skill or experience), be prepared for criticism. Just imagine what Googlers told Brin about his space elevator idea:

- *Don't you have better things to do?*
- *Aren't there better ways to go to space?*
- *Elevators have cables and pulleys. That won't work in space.*

When this happens, the correct answer isn't a defensive "Nuh-uh" or an angry "You try it then."

Instead:

- Acknowledge the criticism.
- Be factual.
- Offer to resolve the situation

Criticism frustrates us. Sometimes we are our toughest critic! When I get frustrated, I try to remind myself: let my frustration be my fascination. That is, set aside the emotions and feelings towards those that criticize me. Move instead toward the fact-based present and try to see the beauty in what I'm experiencing. And for that last boost of confidence, I recall Teddy Roosevelt's "Man in the Arena" quote:

"It is not the critic who counts; not the man who points out how the strong man stumbles, or where the doer of deeds could have done them better. The credit belongs to the man who is actually in the arena, whose face is marred by dust and sweat and blood; who strives valiantly; who errs, who comes short again and again, because there is no effort without error and shortcoming; but who does actually strive to do the deeds; who knows great enthusiasms, the great devotions; who spends himself in a worthy cause; who at the best knows in the end the triumph of high achievement, and who at the worst, if he fails, at least fails while daring greatly, so that his place shall never be with those cold and timid souls who neither know victory nor defeat."

16 Embrace Cannibalism

In business, product cannibalism is the concept that introducing a new product will reduce demand for similar products made by the same company. Companies fear cannibalism because they do not want to hurt profits, sales, or market share.

Steve Jobs, for example, was very comfortable with product cannibalism. He didn't hesitate to introduce the iPhone, even though it cut into sales of his then-popular iPod. And back in the 1980s, Apple colleagues felt Jobs was reckless in introducing the Mac because it threatened the budding and profitable Apple II computer business.

Most companies don't have Jobs' penchant for product cannibalism. For example, Kodak developed and killed their digital camera offering in 1975 – a whopping 15 years before the digital camera category became popular – because Kodak did not want to eat into their profitable film business.

I say embrace your inner Steve Jobs. Reject that fear. Cannibalize your products. Cannibalism is about giving customers what they want. Customer delight is arguably the most important goal for any company, which is the most constructive, optimistic way for us to think about cannibalism.

All the times I've turned aside my fear of decreased profits, I've found the actual cannibalization impact is not as bad as I feared. If anything, I've always found that my overall profits have increased.

And here's one last thought: it's far better for you to cannibalize your own products rather than letting a competitor do so. Here's why: you'll get a chance to retain your customers. Owning that customer relationship is key. Lose them to your competitors, and you'll have to do the hard work of re-acquiring them again.

What's Next

Thanks for reading! First and foremost, I would love to hear from you. Please send questions, comments, typos, and edits to: lewis@impactinterview.com.

Also, email me if you're interested in having my company come to your organization and lead an all-day workshop based on the ESTEEM Method™. The workshop is an opportunity for your organization to experience ESTEEM™ beyond this book. We will lead your organization through a series of valuable, interactive, and fun group exercises. Participants will have a chance to:

- Apply the ESTEEM Method™
- Speed up learning with a critical in-person feedback loop
- Build a plan on how to successfully master ESTEEM™

Next, your journey does not end here. Continue your journey by:

1. Searching on Google for "Lewis C. Lin Slack group"
2. Signing up for that Slack group

3. Continuing the discussion on the Slack channel: #pm-career-talk

In this Slack channel, we'll discuss the book, share tips, and help each other as we progress in our PM careers.

Finally, I have a favor to ask you. Please review the book on Amazon. Whether you loved or hated the book, your review can help me improve subsequent editions of *Be the Greatest Product Manager Ever.*

Book reviews also play an important in promoting my book to a larger audience, which will turn give me a bigger opportunity to create better interview preparation materials for you in the future.

Thank you for reading. May you be the greatest ever.

CHAPTER 9

Appendix

Exhibit 1. How Product Managers Spend Their Time

Typical time spent by product managers,
average % of time spent on each activity across respondents

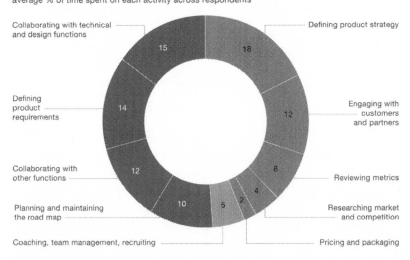

Collaborating with technical and design functions — 15

Defining product strategy — 18

Defining product requirements — 14

Engaging with customers and partners — 12

Collaborating with other functions — 12

Reviewing metrics — 8

Planning and maintaining the road map — 10

Researching market and competition — 4

Coaching, team management, recruiting — 5, 2

Pricing and packaging

McKinsey&Company | **Source:** McKinsey Product Management Index

Source: McKinsey & Company

Acknowledgments

A big thank you goes to everyone involved with this book. I couldn't have done this without your feedback, thoughts, and brainstorming. If I left out any of you, I apologize for the inadvertent exclusion.

Abbie Austin	Jamie Hui
Aqil Pasha	Kaitlin Hung
Arvin Dwarka	Kathy Paceley
Bessie Chu	Maitrayee Goswami
Bonny Lai	Nicole Tang
Declan Nishiyama	Stephanie Chan
Eran Lewis	Taylor Hirth
Jacky Liang